THE YOUNG PERSON'S
GUIDE TO LIVING ISLAM

Published by Tughra Books
345 Clifton Ave., Clifton,
NJ, 07011, USA

www.tughrabooks.com

Library of Congress Cataloging-in-Publication Data Available

Translated by Zaineb Mahmout

ISBN: 978-1-59784-249-5

Printed by
Görsel Dizayn Ofset, Istanbul - Turkey

THE YOUNG PERSON'S
GUIDE TO LIVING ISLAM

Aslı Kaplan

TUGHRA
BOOKS
New Jersey

CONTENTS

Part V
FASTING: HALF OF PATIENCE

Part VI
CHARITY: THE BRIDGE OF THE RELIGION

Part VII
HAJJ: HOLY JOURNEY TO THE HOUSE OF GOD

APPENDIX

In the Name of Allah, the All-Merciful, the All-Compassionate

PREFACE

Recognition of the Creator, faith in His existence and unity is the greatest privilege, the most delightful experience of a human's life. Faith is strongly interrelated with worship, and worship is both a spiritual nourishment and protection of faith; therefore, if a human is deprived of worship, then faith weakens gradually with each day that passes.

Worship is submission to God the Creator of the entire existence; worship is obeying His commands and prohibitions. It is pursuing life with the aim of obtaining the pleasure of God, while avoiding Satan's evil traps and the egoistic pleasures and ambitions of our own desires. A person who experiences the tranquility of fulfilling the duties and obligations to God will in turn be a spiritually sound and responsible human. Worship disciplines the soul against adverse emotions namely selfishness and egoism, emotions which eventually lead the human soul to conceit, arrogance, and pride. Worship constantly reminds us the grandeur of God the Almighty.

Obtaining the pleasure of God is the most excellent achievement of human worship, and those successful in attaining Divine pleasure are blessed in both this world and the hereafter. Could there possibly be a greater reward for any human?

Performing our duty of worship to perfection depends on accurate knowledge of what should be done in certain circumstances and conditions. This book is a form of guidance for the youth of the present in their everyday lives, a compilation of useful information relating to the various forms of worship with informative explanations defined in an understandable manner. This guide for youth today was compiled in accordance with various works accepted by Islamic scholars as a primary source of knowledge. It was prepared with color pictures and illustrations of every stage of performing the rituals of purification and daily prayers. With sincere aspiration and prayer that this will be a means of knowledge to all its readers...

PUBLISHER'S NOTE

This guide for youth has been prepared for the English speaking readers who are not very familiar with the Arabic script. We have provided in this guide some of the short *sûrah*s from the Qur'ân as well as the selected prayers in Arabic along with their interpretation in English. The recitation of certain prayers and some portion of the Qur'ân is obligatory while performing various acts and forms of Islamic worship, especially in the daily prayers. Therefore, it is essential for the Muslim youth to be familiar with basic Islamic terms and expressions and pronounce various Arabic prayers and Qur'anic verses in a correct manner.

In this work, the Islamic terms, certain prayers, and Qur'anic verses are transliterated in the Latin alphabet in order for the English speaking readers to pronounce them reasonably accurately. Readers are further encouraged to learn and practice the correct Arabic pronunciation with the help of a teacher so that they can pronounce the religious terms with perfect accuracy and recite the selected prayers and Qur'anic verses without fault or erroneous dialectic influence.

Aiming to meet the practical need of the non-Arabic speakers in their daily worship, the scholarly and cumbersome use of symbols and diacritical marks for religious terms and expressions has been avoided in this guide for the youth. While rendering various Islamic terms, supplications, and Qur'anic verses, however, we have used as few diacritical marks as are required to aid the correct pronunciation for the English-speaking readers. Other than the macron, which is a diacritical mark placed over a vowel to indicate that the vowel is long, only the diacritics for the *hamza* (') and the *'ayn* (') are used in the transliteration of Arabic terms and expressions. The symbols representing the *hamza*, which is the sign used in Arabic orthography representing a glottal stop, and the *'ayn* may be considered too similar. Therefore, the readers should pay extra attention that the *hamza* is shown by an apostrophe ('), as in the expressions *Qur'ân* and *wudû'*, and the *'ayn* by a single opening quotation mark (') in this guide. The *'ayn* can be described as a violent, tense pharyngeal voiced fricative. While articulating this sound, as in the expressions *'Iyd*, *'Asr*, and *A'ûdhu-Basmala*, for instance, the passage of breath is blocked deep in the throat by constricting the muscles near the Adam's apple, then suddenly opened under pressure and with the vocal chords in action.

Usually, English transliterations of the Arabic script ignore the occasional assimilation of the Arabic definite article, *al*. For the convenience of the novice readers, however, the unpronounced *l* is removed in all the transliterations in this book; instead, the sound of the *l* in *al* is assimilated into the sounds *d, n, r, s, sh, t,* and *z* when it is joined to a noun with a hyphen as in the following examples: "*as-salâmu 'alaykum*", "*at-tashahhud*", and "*Salâtuz-Zuhr*."

Finally, this book is accessible to every Muslim youth, regardless of the Islamic schools they follow. Though it is mainly based on the Hanafi jurisprudence, we have made occasional mention in the text some of the variations available in other Islamic schools.

WHY DO WE WORSHIP?

Worship

The seven heavens and the earth, and whoever is therein, glorify Him. There is nothing that does not glorify Him with His praise (proclaiming that He alone is God, without peer or partner, and all praise belongs to Him exclusively), but you cannot comprehend their glorification. Surely He is (despite what His servants have deserved from Him) All-Clement, All-Forgiving. (Isrâ 17:44)

All of Existence Worships God

And your Lord inspired the bee: "Take for yourself a dwelling-place in the mountains, and in the trees, and in what they (human beings) may build and weave. Then eat of all the fruits, and returning with your loads follow the ways your Lord has made easy for you." There comes forth from their bellies a fluid of varying color, wherein is health for human beings. Surely in this there is a sign for people who reflect. (Nahl 16:68–69)

As revealed in chapter An-Nahl of the holy Qur'ân, God the Almighty created bees to produce honey, just as He created every other existence on earth with a purpose. The whole existence, everything in the entire universe was designed and created with such magnificence and harmonic precision. God ascribed every creation on earth with a specific duty and rendered this duty a form of worship. The bees that make honey, the cow that provides milk, the trees that produce oxygen, and the sun that provides heat to the universe are all fulfilling the duty of worship. The Owner and Creator of the entire existence revealed in the Qur'ân:

The seven heavens and the earth, and whoever is therein, glorify Him. There is nothing that does not glorify Him with His praise, but you cannot comprehend their glorification. Surely He is All-Clement, All-Forgiving. (Isrâ 17:44)

The whole of creation, everything on earth ranging from the tiniest grain to the stars in the Heavens, whether animate or inanimate, continuously fulfills the duties assigned by the Creator to perfection. If every existence fulfills its specific duty and continuously glorifies the Creator, without doubt it is totally unacceptable and illogical that humans, a creation fashioned in the most excellent form and bestowed with innumerous blessings by their Creator, can neglect their duty of worship and glorification.

God the Almighty provided us with heat and energy from the sun, and He blessed us with the means of breathing in the oxygen we depend on in every moment of our lives. He created us with eyes that give us sight, ears that provide us with hearing, and a brain that enables us to think. God adorned the entire universe with unlimited blessings, but the greatest blessing of all is being created as a mindful human. God the Almighty created humans as the most honorable, and in every aspect the most excellent of the entire existence; He created humans as His vicegerents on earth. The only thing He asks from us in return for all these blessings is our devotion and worship.

Worship is submission to God, obeying the Divine commands and restrictions, and living every aspect of our lives to please the Creator, not to satisfy our own desires or the evil commands of Satan. Worship is the most excellent means of expressing our gratitude, the means of showing affection and glorification for all the blessings the Creator bestowed upon us. The greatest accomplishment of worship is gaining the pleasure of God. When a human obtains God's pleasure, he attains contentment in both this world and in the world beyond, what more could a person possibly desire in life?

Worship Reminds Us That We Are Servants

The most excellent aspect of a person's life is recognizing and familiarizing ourselves with the Creator and believing in the existence and unity of God. Faith is strongly related to human worship. Worship both nourishes the soul with spiritual awareness and protects the soul from evil. Human faith is dependent on worship, so the more we worship and gratify the Lord, the stronger our faith becomes, and without worship, faith gradually weakens every passing day.

Our worldly duties and activities constantly occupy and very often distance us from the Creator. However, when we turn to Him in worship and glorification, we sense His presence, a feeling of contentment which brings us even closer to the Lord. Every time we stand before Him in worship, we are reminded of God's affection that He is with us in every moment of our lives. Our hearts are protected from evil thoughts and our bodies guarded from sin, and whenever we do feel the desire to sin, the spiritual awareness we obtain from worship and glorification of the Lord reminds our conscience: "Beware of your actions! Your Lord sees all that you do, never offend or displease Him, for His affection and benevolence is sufficient for you!"

Worship of any kind, whether this is praying, fasting, or reciting the Qur'ân, awakens us to our duty towards God. A human who worships God, recognizes everything acquired in life as a blessing, "a gift from the Creator," and constantly praises the Lord for His endless generosity. As those who follow their egoistic desires and listen to the whisperings of Satan boast of their world-

ly achievements due to utter arrogance and pride, those who worship God concern themselves with their standing in the sight of God for the sake of their lives in this world and the hereafter. A worshipper learns self discipline and makes every effort to maintain faith. A devout servant strives with the aspiration of continuing to live a life of faith and servitude. God the Almighty revealed in the Qur'ân:

> Do not turn your face from people in scornful pride, nor move on earth haughtily. Surely God does not love anyone proud and boastful.
> (Luqmân 31:18)

A human who lives in the contentment and bliss of fulfilling the duty of servitude will be granted with a sound spiritual understanding. Worship is a form of spiritual discipline that eliminates evil emotions from the soul, emotions that would eventually turn into empty pride, arrogance and vaingloriousness, while constantly reminding us that God is the All-Great, the All-Powerful.

The Obligation and Conditions of Worship

Fulfilling the duty of worship in the most excellent manner requires knowledge of what should be done in certain circumstances. But before we proceed to learn the conditions of worship, it may be beneficial to learn specific concepts and terms used to convey various aspects of worship. This section is dedicated to explaining these terms found in later sections of the book.

What does accountable mean?

According to the Islamic faith, a person who is 'accountable' is one who is responsible for fulfilling the duty of obeying the commands of God and refraining from the prohibitions prescribed in the Divine Law. According to Islamic law, the sins of those who are not accountable or responsible for fulfilling these duties are not recorded as sins. This is the difference between those who are and those who are not responsible for their actions. Our good deeds and actions are recorded from a very young age, whereas sins are recorded from the day we reach the age that we become responsible for our actions; this is known as adolescence or puberty.

What are the conditions of accountability?

The conditions that deem a person responsible for obeying the commands and prohibitions of God are that he or she must:

- ◆ Be a Muslim
- ◆ Be a sane human
- ◆ Have reached puberty

God the Almighty prescribed a specific period from the time when a Muslim is born until he reaches puberty to acquire the necessary religious education, and in a display of His mercy and compassion, He does not hold humans responsible for their sins or evil actions during this period of childhood.

What does puberty mean?

Puberty or adolescence is the period when a youth grows out of childhood, when bio-logically it becomes possible for a boy to be a father, and physically possible for a girl to be a mother. Puberty in boys begins when they experience sexual discharge during the night. The sign of a girl reach-ing puberty is when she begins to men-struate. Menstruation is regular monthly bleeding from the womb commonly

known as the monthly period or the monthly cycle. According to most Islamic scholars, the age of puberty for girls is defined from between the age of 9–15, and for boys it is usually from the age of 12–15. According to the Islamic faith, those who have reached the age of 15 but have not yet experienced the signs of puberty, namely sexual discharge or the menstrual cycle have nevertheless reached puberty. There are various duties that every Muslim is obligated to execute upon reaching puberty.

What is a fard, or obligatory, duty?

These are the duties clearly prescribed by God and deemed obligatory upon every Muslim, namely the five daily prayers, the fast, giving prescribed alms, and so on. We gain reward for performing these obligatory duties; however, neglecting these duties is a huge sin. A human who rejects a *fard*, or obligatory duty, is rejecting one of the Divine commands and disobeying God and is therefore rejecting faith. The obligatory duties are divided into two categories, referred to as *fard al-'ayn* and *fard al-kifâyah*. *Fard al-'ayn* defines the duties every individual

Muslim is required to perform according to the Islamic faith. These are duties that are a prescribed obligation of the individual, duties that do not cease to be the duty of individuals when carried out by others, for example the prayer and fasting. *Fard al-kifâyah* is a duty that is not prescribed upon the individual alone, but incurred upon Muslims as a (local) community. This obligation is fulfilled for all Muslims when performed by a few members of that community. However, if the entire community abstains from performing this communal obligation, all Muslims in that community are deemed responsible, and all will be classified as sinners. For example the funeral prayer, if the funeral prayer is performed by a group of the Muslim community, it ceases to be obligatory upon all, but if the whole community abstains from performing the funeral prayer, the entire community is responsible and considered sinners.

What does wâjib mean?

These are duties that have been prescribed, but evidence portraying these as obligatory is not as decisive as it is for the *fard* duties. For example, offering a sacrificial animal and performing the *witr* and the *'Iyd* (religious festive day) prayers are considered *wâjib* in the Hanafi School. The reason for this distinction in the Hanafi School is the strength of the evidence that exists to establish the obligatory nature of the worship. While the evidence for a *fard* is decisive in both its authenticity and implication, a *wâjib*, in the Hanafi School, is that which has been proved by presumptive evidence in either its textual implication or transmission. Though the reward for a *fard* (obligatory) duty is higher than the reward for fulfilling a duty classified as *wâjib* (necessary), the Islamic ruling of *wâjib* is the same as the *fard* duty. If performed the individual gains reward, but if abandoned he or she is committing a sin.

What is Sunnah?

This is the general term used for the words God's Messenger conveyed, his behavior, habits, and his approval on certain subjects. His approval usually meant the Prophet's practice of remaining silent at the time of an incident or when later explained to him by other members of the community. In brief, the Prophet's traditions and way of life on a whole is collectively referred to as the *Sunnah* of the Prophet.

The *Sunnah* of the Prophet Muhammad, peace and blessings be upon him, is divided into two categories, the *sunnah mu'akkadah* and *sunnah ghayr mu'akkadah*. *Sunnah mu'akkadah* refers to the traditions that the Prophet continuously practiced and very rarely abandoned, for example the *Sunnah* prayers of the morning, noon, and evening prayers.

Sunnah ghayr mu'akkadah are the traditions that the Prophet practiced most of the time and abandoned occasionally; for example, the first *Sunnah* prayers of the late noon and night prayers.

The *sunnah ghayr mu'akkadah* also includes the traditions of the Prophet's good manners and actions, his manner of dressing, his eating and drinking habits, his manner of sitting, and even how he walked. Although practicing these traditions of the Prophet bears great reward and abandoning these *sunnah*s is not considered a sin, those who choose not to practice the traditions of the Prophet may be deprived of his intercession on the Day of Judgment.

Why is practicing the Sunnah so important?

The Prophet's Sunnah constitutes an important dimension the Islamic faith. The best way of Islamic living can be found in every aspect of the life of the Prophet, who is *"an excellent example (for everybody) to follow"* (Ahzâb 33:21). Truly observing the sunnah, or practices, of the Prophet means doing as he did in not only the obligatory practices of Islam but also the non-obligatory matters. If the Prophetic traditions were made compulsory, without doubt every one of us would have repeatedly sinned hundreds of times every day. For example, washing our hands before and after a meal, eating and drinking with our right hand, brushing our teeth, praying before going to sleep and on waking up, and being kind to others are all *sunnah*s, or practices of the Prophet. These are just a few of the hundreds of the Prophetic traditions that all of us may perform daily of our own choice, but can you imagine if all the traditions were deemed compulsory? It is quite likely that we would not have been able to practice every one of the *sunnah*s with the care and accuracy required, so often we would probably have abandoned these obligatory duties and therefore sinned throughout the whole day.

It is evident that God Almighty deemed the Prophet's traditions not obligatory, but optional due to His compassion and mercy for humans, His desire to establish ease for His devoted servants, and in order not to make our religion difficult to practice. The *Sunnah as-saniyyah* is the actions and behavior of Prophet Muhammad, peace and blessings be upon him, his way of life. How could having such an excellent character, a polite manner of speaking and kindness like his possibly be classified as insignificant?

The Sunnah of the Prophet is like a compass that guides Muslims in every aspect of their lives, continuously indicating the direction of the path of excellence and in total accuracy. The conduct of the Prophet who said, "My Lord educated me," the most excellent behavior that he continued to display throughout the course of his life, was the course of conduct chosen by the Creator. Whoever neglects this guidance to the path of excellence will stray towards destruction.

A person must comply with the *Sunnah as-saniyyah* to obtain affection for God, for we must live and behave in a manner that pleases Him in order to be blessed with sincere devotion and affection for God. The most excellent, most perfect morals and exceptional example of humanity was portrayed in Prophet Muhammad, peace and blessings be upon him. A person who is heedless to the Sunnah will be deprived of the affection of God and of His Messenger. The Prophet related in one of his traditions: "Whoever adheres to my Sunnah during the time of corruption will be blessed with the reward of a hundred martyrs," clearly portraying the importance of abiding by the Prophet's traditions.

In many verses of the Qur'ân, the Prophet was defined as the most excellent example for mankind:

Assuredly you have in God's Messenger an excellent example to follow. (Ahzâb 33:21)

You are surely of a sublime character, and do act by a sublime pattern of conduct. (Qalam 68:4)

Say (to them, O Messenger): "If you indeed love God, then follow me, so that God will love you and forgive you your sins." God is All-Forgiving, All-Compassionate. (Âl 'Imrân 3:31)

There has come to you (O people) a Messenger from among yourselves; extremely grievous to him is your suffering; full of concern for you is he, and for the believers, full of pity and compassion. (Tawbah 9:128)

Halâl

This is what is lawful or permitted according to the Islamic law—anything that is not prohibited in the Islamic faith.

Harâm

This includes anything clearly determined to be forbidden by God; for example gambling, lying, drinking alcohol, slander, gossip, and abusing the rights of others. It is a sin to participate in anything forbidden by Islamic law, and those who abandon that which is prohibited will be rewarded. Whoever considers what God prescribed forbidden as *halâl*, or lawful, will be denying faith.

Makruh

These are actions that have not been clearly defined as prohibited, but they are actions that are disliked or disapproved of in the Islamic faith. The character of the action and the conditions or situation in which an action was performed can determine whether the action is a sin. Nevertheless, even the most insignificant of sins should be considered important.

The minor sins we may consider trivial accumulate and eventually transform to major sins, just like the thin threads that combine to form a thick rope. These are a few examples of actions considered *makruh* or unadvisable in Islam: wasting water while performing ablution or purification for the prayer, yawning during the prayer, cleaning oneself with the right hand after the call of nature, and performing the prayers while in need of using the toilet.

The reason these actions are not prohibited in Islam stems from the Creator's compassion towards His servants... His endless Mercy has protected us all from constantly committing sin.

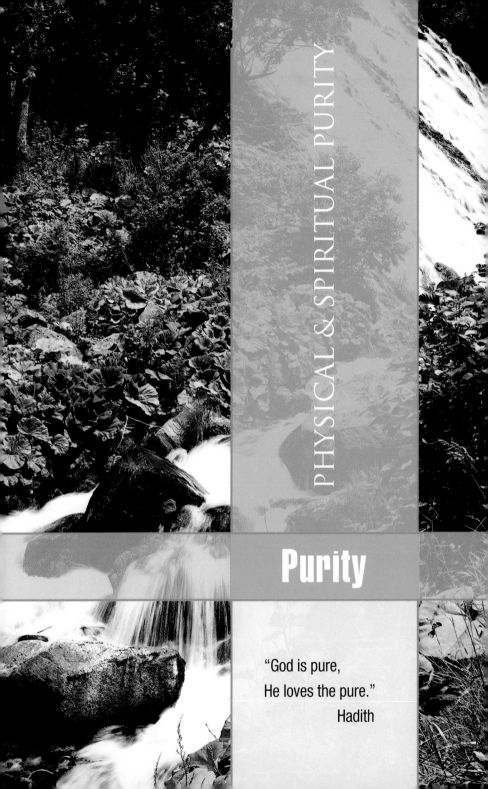

PHYSICAL & SPIRITUAL PURITY

Purity

"God is pure,
He loves the pure."
Hadith

Islam Is the Religion of Purity

O ur religion orders us to be in a state of purity when we worship. In Islam, a religion which gives great importance to cleanliness, purity is like the spiritual essence of worship. In the Qur'ân God revealed: *"God loves those who strive to purify themselves"* (Tawbah 9:108). And with his words "God is pure, and He only accepts those who are pure," the Prophet emphasized the importance of purity in Islam.

To obtain the pleasure and love of God, a Muslim must be physically clean, and the soul purified of evil thoughts and spiritual impurities. This is why Muslims must give importance to cleanliness in every aspect of their lives. Purification is a condition of the acceptance of any form of worship. For example we must perform ablutions, the ritual of purification before the prayer. Prayer (*salâh*) is not accepted without purification. In addition to physical purification, the area where we pray must also be clean to ensure the acceptance of the prayer. Then there is spiritual purity which is even more important than the physical purification. Spiritual purity is only feasible if we purify our thoughts and emotions of evil and transform our spirituality accordingly to please the Creator.

What is tahârah? What are the different kinds of tahârah?

The meaning of the word *tahârah* is purification. According to the Islamic faith, *tahârah* is purifying oneself of major impurities namely the physical and spiritual impurities which prevent the acceptance of worship. There are two types of purification, or *tahârah*:

1. Purification from the *najâsah* (material impurities)
2. Purification from the *hadath* (ritual impurities)

What is the purification of najâsah?

Najâsah is the state of material impurity, and *najis* is the name given to the substance of impurity which deems us physically unclean. Purification of these impurities entails the cleansing of the body or clothing from anything which is regarded as impure in Islam.

What is the purification of hadath?

Hadath is the state of impurity which religiously prevents us from performing worship: lack of ablution and the conditions in which *ghusl* (bathing) is required; for example, wet dream, the completion of a woman's monthly cycle, and the bleeding due to childbirth. By performing the ritual of purification of ablution or bathing, we are cleansed of this impurity. The reasons and situations that require ablution or bathing will be explained in greater depth in the section of the book dedicated to the purification from the *hadath*, or ritual impurities.

Purification of Material Impurities

Najâsah, or material impurities, are divided in two groups: those that impede the performance of the daily prayers and those that do not impede performing the prayers. The first: fecal excrement, urine, blood, semen, and discharge of humans and animals whose meat is prohibited, and the excretion of poultry namely chickens, goose, and ducks whose meat is permitted to eat in Islam. These forms of impurities are known as *najâsat al-ghalîzah*, or heavy impurity. We must ensure that neither our bodies nor our clothing come into contact with these impurities. Among these impurities: an amount of solid impurity weighing 2,80 grams (0,10 of an ounce) or less or liquid impurity no larger than the palm of the human hand does not invalidate the prayer. If any amount exceeding that stated comes in contact with the body or clothing, the impurity must be removed and cleaned before praying. Impure blood is the blood which flows from the bodies of humans and animals. However, any blood which remains in the meat and veins, the blood remaining inside and outside the liver and hearts of animals sacrificed according to the Islamic regulations, and the blood of flees, lice, grasshoppers and flies all do not invalidate the prayer.

The second form of impurity is the excretion and urine of animals prescribed *halâl*, namely horses, goats, cattle, buffalo, and camels, and the excretion of birds whose meat is forbidden to eat in Islam. These forms of impurity are called *najâsat al-khafîfah*, or light impurity. The prayer is valid if one forth or less of the body or clothing comes into contact with this form of impurity, but invalid if the amount exceeds that stated.

Although our religion permits us to pray if we have come in contact with a specific amount of the defined impurities, this is to relieve any difficulty of performing our duties of worship and is only in the case of necessity. In accordance with our faith, it is more desirable to go before the Creator in a state of total purity.

The Means of Purification

Anything that has come in contact with an impurity should be purified by washing or wiping with clean water. Washing the area polluted with the impure substance three times is sufficient to cleanse the body or clothing. If a garment has come in contact with an impurity, washing the garment at least three times and wringing it each time so that the least possible amount of water remains is sufficient. If the polluted area is on a larger or thicker item that cannot be wrung, for example a carpet, washing the item three times with an interval each time it is washed until the water ceases to drip is sufficient to cleanse it of the impurity. Solid items which do not absorb the impurity, for example glass, marble and porcelain, can be cleaned by wiping, scraping, or scrubbing with a clean cloth and water.

Purification of the Body according to the Sunnah

In one of the hadith, the Prophet said: "It is a duty that every Muslim owes to God to take a bath (at least) every seven days," expressing the importance of cleansing the body. In addition to washing and purifying the whole body of dirt and sweat, there are also specific areas of the body that we should wash more frequently. The hair, the armpits, and genital areas should be washed often, and the hair that grows under the arms and around the groin area should be removed on a regular basis.

Every Muslim must cut both the finger and toe nails frequently and make a habit of brushing the teeth and keeping the nose clean. It is more desirable to cut the hair or nails when the body is in a state of purity.

Ablution – The Purification of Spiritual Impurities

The word *wudî'*, or ablution, literally means water used to wash the hands and face. As a religious term described in the Qur'ân and traditions of the Prophet, ablution is purification of certain organs of the body with water or by performing *tayammum* (purification using sand or dust when water is not available).

Ablution is the means of physical and spiritual protection. A Muslim who performs ablution at least five times a day becomes accustomed to cleanliness which protects him from various cases of illness. The ritual purification is the means of expiating minor sins and conveys excellence and contentment to the soul. A person who regularly performs ablutions, or who is in the state of ritual purity at all times, will be more capable of guarding himself from evil thoughts and sin. The Prophet explained the virtues of ritual purification in one of the hadith: "Whoever performs the ritual of purification as prescribed, and then prays as prescribed, his past minor sins will be forgiven."

The ritual ablution was deemed obligatory in this verse of the Qur'ân:

> O you who believe! When you rise up for the Prayer, wash your faces and your hands up to the elbows, and lightly rub your heads (with water), and (wash) your feet up to the ankles. (Mâedah 5:6)

What are the fard (obligatory) acts of ablution?

There are four obligatory acts of ablution:

1. Washing the whole face, from the hairline to below the chin once.

2. Washing the hands and arms including the elbows once.

3. Wiping one fourth of the head with wet hands, also known as *masah*.

4. Washing the feet including the ankles once.

What are the sunnah acts of ablution?

It is Sunnah to perform the following acts of ablution:

1. Cleaning the teeth with a miswak or toothbrush before performing the ablution.

2. Reciting the *A'ûdhu-Basmala*[1] at the beginning of ablution.

3. Proclaiming the intention of performing the ablution.

4. Washing the hands up to the wrists three times.

5. Washing the limbs necessary in ablution three times each.

6. Rinsing the mouth and breathing water into the nostrils three times.

7. Performing the ablution in accordance with the order prescribed in the Qur'ân.

8. Washing the right limbs first.

9. Wiping the head from the forehead to the neck with wet hands.

---

1   *A'ûdhu-Basmala* is the Arabic expression of *A'ûdhu billâhi min ash-shaytânir-rajîm Bismillahir-Rahmânir-Rahîm*. It means "I seek refuge in God from Satan eternally rejected (from God's Mercy). In the Name of God, the All-Merciful, the All-Compassionate."

10. Wiping the two ears and neck with wet hands.

11. While washing the hands and feet, beginning with the tips of the toe and fingertips.

Although abandoning any of the sunnah acts does not invalidate the ablution, it does reduce the reward for performing a sunnah of the Prophet. Therefore, when we perform the rituals of purification, we should follow the Prophet's actions as an example just as we do in every aspect of our lives and worship.

Important Matters to Consider While Performing Ablution

1. Ensuring that no area of the limbs washed during ablution remains dry.

2. Removing any substance that could prevent water being absorbed into the skin or from coming into contact with the nails, such as clay, paint, and nail varnish.

3. Henna does not invalidate ablution as it does not prevent water from coming in contact with the skin or the nails.

4. While performing ablution, moving any rings on the fingers to ensure water reaches the skin beneath the rings.

5. Ensuring that the feet are washed up to the ankles.

6. Washing between the toes.

7. If any of the limbs to be washed during ablution has a wound or condition which may be harmed by water, wiping over the wound with wet hands is sufficient. However, it is unnecessary to wipe the wound if this too can cause harm.

8. If a wound or a limb of the body is covered with a bandage, and removing the bandage may be harmful, wiping over the bandage with wet hands is enough.

9. Although not abiding by the prescribed order of washing the organs does not invalidate the ablution, it does reduce the rewards for performing the purification.

10. Pausing while performing the ritual of purification is an undesirable act, but it does not invalidate the ablution.

11. A person who has lost the whole or part of a limb that must be washed during ablution should wash the existing part of the limb.

What invalidates ablution?

1. Passing urine or fecal excrement.

2. Passing gas.

3. The discharge of blood or pus which flows from any part of the body.

4. Vomiting a mouthful of vomit or more (even if vomited in small amounts at a time).

5. Sleeping while lying or leaning against something.

6. Fainting.

7. Intoxication.

8. Laughing aloud during the prayer to the extent that others can hear.

What does not invalidate ablution?

1. Vomiting less than a mouthful of vomit.

2. Emitting phlegm.

3. Dozing in the sitting or kneeling position while not leaning against something.

4. Crying and laughing aloud (not during the prayer). If crying is because of some divine or religious thoughts, it is desirable and certainly does not harm ablution or the prayers.

5. Smiling during the prayer.

6. Cutting the hair or nails.

7. Laughing during the prayer to the extent that others cannot hear invalidates the prayer but does not invalidate ablution.

8. If any blood or discharge of pus from the body is no larger than prick of a needle and does not flow or spread, ablution is not invalidated.

What is not permitted without performing ablution?

1. Prayer (*salâh*)

2. Performing the *tawaf*

3. Handling the Qur'ân.

The Qur'ân can only be touched or handled without having ablution (*wudû'*) if it is covered or held by a clean item. The important point here is that the cover should not be attached to the Qur'ân itself. Other than the glorious book of the Qur'ân, however, various religious books that contain verses of the Qur'ân can be held and read without performing ablutions. Though having ablution is a must to hold and read the Qur'ân, memorized verses of the Qur'ân can be recited without ablution.

Why is being in constant state of purity such a virtue?

Being in a constant state of purity is a means of great reward and spiritual blessings. A Muslim can perform acts of excellence and any form of worship at any time while in a constant state of purity. Prophet Muhammad, peace and blessings be upon him,

How Is Ablution Performed?

While making the ablution, there are both the fard and sunnah acts of ablution, as well as other important matters that should be considered while performing ablution; the succession of performing the ablution is as follows:

First you begin by making the intention for ablution: "I intend to perform the ritual of ablution for the sake of God." You do not have to say the intention aloud; affirming the intention in the heart is sufficient for fulfilling the condition of the intention for ablution.

After making the intention, recite A'ūdhu-Basmala and then wash both hands, up to and including the wrists, rubbing each finger thoroughly. Rings should be moved or removed to enable the water to cleanse the entire hand.

Cup water in the right hand and rinse out the mouth three times. Then take water from your cupped right hand into the nostrils three times, using the left to blow the water back out.

Wash your face three times with both hands, from ear to ear and from the top of the forehead to the chin.

Wash your right arm up to (and including) the elbow three times.

Then wash your left arm up to (and including) the elbow three times.

Wipe at least a quarter of your head once with a wet hand.

Wipe your ear-holes with either your forefinger or little finger, and the outer ear with your thumb; wipe the back and sides of your neck with the back of both hands.

First wash the right and then the left foot, up to the ankles, making sure water goes between the toes.

It is recommended that the *shahâdah* be recited when the ablution is completed. It is also recommended that the individual does not talk but prays to God and offers greetings to the Prophet while performing ablution.

said that the angels pray and ask forgiveness for whoever is in a state of purity and performed ablution before going to bed. Purification is so important that it was reported that whoever is in a state of purity at all times:

◆ Will be blessed with rewards continuously.

◆ His every limb glorifies God constantly.

◆ Is protected by the angels during the night from anything that may cause harm.

◆ Will constantly be under the protection of his Creator.

Ghusl: The Complete Ablution

What is the meaning of ghusl?

Ghusl means washing the whole body (bathing). The Islamic meaning of *ghusl* is washing the entire body with clean water, ensuring that no area of the body remains dry. Another word for *ghusl* is the full ablution.

When must ghusl be performed?

There are three conditions of impurity that require *ghusl*, or full ablution:

1. The state of major impurity (*junub*). One of the states of major impurity is the emission of semen from the male sexual organ. This is the ejaculation of semen due to touching and the thought or sight of the opposite sex that sexually arouses a person.

Semen is a white thick substance emitted from the male sexual organ due to sexual lust. If a person who, after experiencing the emission of semen, performs *ghusl* immediately or before urinating and later notices even a tiny drop of semen discharged from the sexual organ, he must repeat the *ghusl* again. *Ghusl* is not necessary if the discharge of semen is not due to sexual lust.

Anyone who experiences the discharge of semen while sleeping must perform *ghusl* even if they cannot remember the wet dream or cause of the discharge. *Ghusl* is not necessary if a person wakes from sleep assuming they are in a state of impurity but sees no mark of semen on either the body or clothing.

Ghusl is not necessary if the emission of *mazi* (a clear, sticky prostatic fluid) occurs; this is emission from the sexual organ which is not due to sexual lust. However, this kind of emission does invalidate ablution. This may be because of the cold, an illness, or even lifting something heavy. On some occasions, a thick white cloudy substance known as *wadi* can sometimes be emitted from the sexual organ after urinating. This invalidates ablution, but does not invalidate *ghusl*. *Ghusl* is also obligatory for any man or woman following sexual intercourse.

2. The second case in which *ghusl* is necessary is due to bleeding after childbirth. This is called *nifas*. Performing *ghusl* is necessary for a woman whose bleeding ceases after the birth of a child.

3. The third case in which *ghusl* is obligatory is following the menstruation of women. *Ghusl* is necessary when the monthly menstrual bleeding of the woman ends. Non-menstrual vaginal bleeding after the completion of the monthly cycle is not, however, considered impure and thus does not necessitate repeating the *ghusl*.

In addition to the situations stated above, performing *ghusl* is necessary for every person who embraces Islam. A woman who embraces Islam during her menstrual period must perform *ghusl* immediately after her monthly cycle ends.

What are the fard (obligatory) acts of performing ghusl?

There are three obligatory acts of performing *ghusl*:

1. Filling and gargling the mouth with water once.

2. Breathing water up into the nostrils once.

3. Washing the entire body so that no area of the body remains dry.

What are the sunnah acts of performing ghusl?

1. Beginning *ghusl* by reciting the *A'ûdhu-Basmala*.

2. Making the intention for performing *ghusl*.

3. Washing the hands up to the wrists and the sexual organ before beginning *ghusl* and then performing the ritual of ablution.

4. Following ablution, washing the head three times, then pouring water over the right, then the left shoulders three times.

Important Matters to Consider While Performing Ghusl

1. Water must reach the roots of the hair and beard.

2. Rings must be removed or moved to enable water to reach beneath the ring, and earrings in pierced ears must be moved so that water enters the holes.

3. It is necessary to cleanse the body of any substance which may prevent water from reaching the skin. Any material which does not absorb water, for instance, paint or nail polish must be completely removed. Coloring substances like henna and ink which do not prevent water from reaching the skin do not affect *ghusl* in any way.

4. If anyone realizes that the nose or mouth was not washed, or a certain part of the body remained dry after performing *ghusl*, washing the specific area is sufficient to validate the *ghusl*. Repeating the bath is not necessary.

5. Removing unwanted hair from the body or cutting the nails when the body is in a state of purity is more appropriate, but this does not affect the validity of the *ghusl* in any way.

How to Perform Ghusl

We begin by making the intention for *ghusl*, "I intend to perform the ritual of purification for the sake of God," and after reciting the *A'ûdhu-Basmala*, the sexual organ is washed to remove any impurities. Following this, the ritual ablution is performed just as it is for the prayer. Then finally the entire body must be washed, preferably rubbed so that no area of the body remains dry.

Only the obligatory acts of the ritual of purification may be executed if the person is short of time. First, by rinsing and gargling the mouth with water and taking water into the nostrils, and then by pouring water over the head, the right and left shoulders, and washing the entire body to ensure that no area remains dry. When water has reached every part the body and the individual is certain that there is no dry area remaining on the body, both the physical and spiritual purification of *ghusl* is complete.

Can we pray after ghusl without performing ablution?

The prayer or any form of worship can be performed without having to perform ablution after *ghusl*, and a person can continue to worship until any of the conditions that invalidate the ablution occurs. If a discharge which usually invalidates ablution, for example blood or urine, is emitted from the body during *ghusl*, the *ghusl* is not invalid. The individual is purified of the major impurity, but cannot perform the prayers or recite the Qur'ân in this state and is therefore required to perform ablution for worship.

What is prohibited in the state of major impurity?

1. Performing the prayer.
2. Reading the Qur'ân.
3. Handling the Qur'ân.
4. Entering a mosque (unless under obligation to do so).
5. Performing *tawaf* (circumambulating) around the Ka'bah.

What is permitted in the state of major impurity?

A person in the state of *junub* (major impurity that necessitates bathing):

1. Can recite the *A'ûdhu-Basmala*.

2. Can hold the Qur'ân with a clean cloth or piece of clothing.

3. Can recite the chapters and verses of the Qur'ân which bear the characteristics of supplication or remembrance, for example *Al-Fâtihah*, *Al-Ikhlâs*, *Âyatul-Kursî*, and with the intention of supplication, may recite the prayers of supplication mentioned in the Hadith.

4. A person in the state of major impurity can recite words of praise and glorification of God, for example *Lâ ilâha illallâh* (There is no deity save God"), *Lâ hawla wa lâ quwwata illâ billah* ("There is no power and no strength save in God"), *Subhân Allâh* ("Glorified is God"), and *Alhamdulillâh* ("All praise belongs to God").

5. The supplication of God's greeting upon the Prophet and his family; in particular, the daily supplications and *dhikr* (remembrance) of God conveyed in the Prophet's traditions can be recited while in the state of major impurity.

6. A person can eat or drink in the state of major impurity, but the hands and mouth should be washed before eating. Those who intend to fast before dawn may eat if they are in the state of major impurity and perform the *ghusl* after they have eaten.

7. A person may sleep in the state of major impurity, on condition that the prayer is not missed.

Tayammum: Purity without Water

What is tayammum?

Tayammum is performing the rituals of purification with clean earth or dust. *Tayammum* is permissible when a person cannot find water, or the water available cannot be used for various reasons. If water is unavailable, *tayammum* can be performed instead of *ghusl*. *Tayammum* performed with the intention of *ghusl* deems a person clean of major impurities.

Tayammum is a special blessing that God bestowed solely upon the Prophet's community—a means of convenience bestowed upon all Muslims. It is the means of purification which enables Muslims to cleanse themselves for the preparation of worship at times when water is not available or under certain conditions when the use of water is not possible. Therefore eliminating any unavoidable aspect which would normally prevent us worshipping the Creator.

When is tayammum permissible?

1. *Tayammum* can be performed when there is insufficient water for ablution or *ghusl* or when the source of water is so far away that it is impossible to obtain.

2. If the use of water will most certainly cause illness, if there is fear of an illness increasing or prolonging due to the use of water, or if performing ablution or *ghusl* with water is forbidden by a qualified doctor.

3. If there is sufficient water to perform ablution or *ghusl*, but there is a possibility that using or obtaining the water will endanger the individual's life or the lives of those close to them.

4. If there is water, but the water is impossible to reach for various reasons; for example, if there is no means of lifting water

from a well, if it is on a high cliff top, or if there is any kind of obstacle preventing the person from reaching the water.

It is every individual's duty to search for or inquire about the availability of water to the best of his or her abilities. Where possible, a person must first ask others regarding the availability of water in surrounding areas.

Some Important Points about Tayammum

1. *Tayammum* can be performed before the time of the prayer, but if is there is any probability of obtaining water before the prayer time expires, it is better to delay performing *tayammum*.

2. It is essential to make the intention for *tayammum*. While starting *tayammum*, it is a must that a separate *tayammum* be performed for each act of worship, even if they are performed one after the other. For instance, if someone who is in a state of impurity that necessitates bathing has to enter the mosque, he performs *tayammum* with the intention of entering the mosque; however, he cannot perform the prayer with the same *tayammum*.

3. Performing *tayammum* is permissible for any person who has wounds on half or the majority of the parts of the body that is necessary to wash during ablution.

4. It is permissible to perform *tayammum* if the greater part of a person's body is covered in wounds.

5. Anyone who does not have the strength to perform ablution alone and has nobody to help with performing ablution may perform *tayammum*.

6. A person who has both or one hand missing and is unable to use water to perform ablution can perform *tayammum*. In such a case, rubbing the face and arms in sand or dust is sufficient to complete the ritual of purification.

What are the fard (compulsory) acts of tayammum?

There are two compulsory acts of performing *tayammum*:

1. To make the intention.

2. Placing both hands on clean soil, sand, or dust twice: The first time, removing any excess dust from the hands and then wiping the entire face with both hands. The second time, wiping the right arm, including the elbow with the left hand, and the left arm, including the elbow with the right hand.

What acts of tayammum are sunnah?

The principle acts which are sunnah while performing *tayammum* are:

1. Reciting the *Basmala* before *tayammum*.

2. Performing *tayammum* according to the prescribed order, for example wiping the face, followed by the arms.

3. Not pausing, or attending any other duty while performing *tayammum*.

What invalidates (breaks) tayammum?

1. The conditions which invalidate ablution or make *ghusl* necessary also invalidates *tayammum*.

2. When water becomes available, or when there is no obstacle or reason preventing a person from using water, *tayammum* becomes invalidated.

3. When the obstacle or reason permitting *tayammum* is no longer valid, or if a person recovers from health problems which initially prevented the use of water, *tayammum* is invalidated.

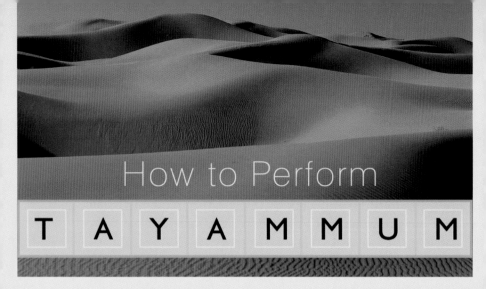

How to Perform
T A Y A M M U M

The person must first recite the *A'ûdhu-Basmala* and make the intention of performing *tayammum* in the heart.

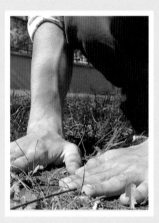 

Then spreading the fingers, he or she must rub both hands on clean soil, sand, or dust which is on a clean surface and then shake or rub the hands to remove any excess dust.

Then the individual must wipe the entire face with both hands and repeat the process of placing the hands on the dust or soil, removing any excess dust again.

Then he or she must wipe the right arm, including the elbow, with the left hand, and the left arm, including the elbow with the right hand, thereby completing *tayammum*, or dry ablution.

MATTERS SPECIFICALLY
REGARDING WOMEN

Haydh, Nifas
& Istihâdha

"Abandon the prayer
when your menses
begins, and when it
ends, perform *ghusl*
(bathing) and then
pray." Hadith

Matters of Concern to Muslim Women

There are three conditions which specifically concern women, *haydh*, *nifas*, and *istihâdha*.

Haydh (Menstruation)

What is haydh?

Haydh is the blood discharged from every healthy woman during a certain age span. The discharge of this blood is usually referred to as menstruation, or the monthly cycle. Menstruation is a condition which specifically concerns women. When young girls experience their first menstruation, they have reached the age of puberty. This is the time when religious duties become obligatory for a Muslim girl.

The impure and toxic substances that accumulate in the body are discarded together with the menstrual blood, which both relieves and revives the body. Therefore, menstruation is not something to fear or to feel disgusted or embarrassed about. These are biological changes that every young girl must experience to become a mother in the later stages of life. This is a condition that should be recognized as a normal process of growing up and, of course the will and a great blessing of God.

Important Matters Regarding Haydh

1. Menstruation begins at the earliest at nine years of age, and it continues at specific times of the month until the age of around fifty five years old. Any bleeding from the womb after the age of fifty five is not classified as menstruation.

2. Menstruation continues for the minimum of three and the maximum ten days every month. Any bleeding that lasts for less than three and more than ten days is not recognized as menstrual bleeding. Both cases are considered as *istihâdha*, which is bleeding due to an illness or abnormality, a subject that we will be describe in more detail later on in the book.

3. The state of purity between two menstruations should be fifteen days or more. Therefore, any bleeding that occurs less than fifteen days after the last monthly cycle ended is not classified as menstrual bleeding.

4. A young girl who experiences bleeding from the womb for the first time must abandon the prayer and fasting. If the bleeding ceases in less than three days, then this is not menstrual bleeding, in which case any prayers or fasts the woman missed during this time must be compensated for.

5. If bleeding from the womb experienced by a young girl lasts for more than three and less than ten days, this is classified

as *haydh*, or menstrual bleeding. The period of bleeding between three and ten days determines the menstrual cycle. For example, if the blood flows and continues until the eighth day, the menstrual cycle is defined as eight days.

6. If the blood flow of a young girl experiencing menstruation for the first time continues for a number of months with no interval, ten days of the month is classified as the menstrual cycle, and twenty days are considered as the period of purity, or free from the menses.

7. The duration of the menstrual cycle of every individual varies. While the duration of some women can be on a regular basis of five, seven, or even nine days each month, the duration of others can vary from month to month.

8. If a woman whose normal menstrual cycle is five days bleeds for six or seven days one month, but the next month returns to the normal cycle of five days, her monthly cycle is classified as five days. However, if a woman, whose menstrual cycle is usually five days bleeds for six days in two consecutive months, then her menstrual cycle is classified as six days.

9. If a woman who usually menstruates for four, five, or six days continues to menstruate for seven, eight, nine, or ten days one month, this will be classified as menstruation only if the bleeding does not exceed the ten days. The person having such an irregular monthly cycle stays away from performing daily prayers for the excess days of menstruation on the condition that the bleeding does not exceed ten days. If the bleeding continues for more than ten days, then her usual monthly cycle is considered as menstruation, and the extended days are classified as *istihâdha*, or bleeding due to abnormality or illness. In which case, any prayers that were not performed during the days of the abnormal bleeding (bleeding exceeding the days of the normal menstruation) must be performed.

10. It is not essential for the blood of menstruation to flow continuously throughout the whole cycle. If there are intervals in the discharge of blood, the bleeding seen during the days of menstruation is classified as menstrual bleeding.

11. The blood discharged during the menstrual period may be red, a dark almost black color, a dark yellowish color, or brown. But whatever the color, any blood discharged according to the stated conditions is classified as menstrual bleeding.

Menstrual bleeding ends when the discharge turns into a pure white colored discharge.

12. If menstrual bleeding begins before a woman has the chance to perform a prayer which has already begun, that particular prayer has become obligatory upon her, and therefore she must perform that prayer when her menses end.

13. A menstruating woman is not considered to be in a state of purity and therefore cannot perform the duty of worship until the menses have ended and she has performed the ritual of purification. As we mentioned earlier in the section of the book dedicated to *ghusl* or bathing due to major impurity, the means of purification when the menstrual bleeding ends is performing *ghusl*. If a woman's menstrual bleeding ends and she has sufficient time to perform *ghusl* and pray before the time for the prayer ends, then she must perform that specific prayer. However if she performs *ghusl* as soon as she ends her menses but does not have enough time to pray before the prescribed time for prayer ends, she is understood as menstruating during the entire duration of that specific prayer and is not therefore expected to perform that prayer.

14. If a woman intends to fast while she is in the state of purity and menstrual bleeding occurs after she begins to fast, the fast is deemed invalid, and she must perform that particular fast and any days of the fast which were missed when the menstrual bleeding ends. If a woman continues to fast regardless of the fast becoming invalid, there is no religious benefit or reward of holding the fast. It is permissible for a woman to eat and drink from the time she sees the menstrual discharge.

15. During the month of Ramadan, if the menstrual bleeding ends before the call for evening prayer, it is not a sin for her to eat and drink before the fast ends even if she has performed *ghusl*.

16. If for any reason a woman assumes that her menses has begun, but sees no actual sign of blood, or the bleeding is obstructed with any substance, she is not classified as menstruating until she actually sees the blood. Menstruation begins from the first sign of menstrual blood.

Why is cleanliness so important during menstruation?

During the period of menstruation, one of the most important factors to consider is hygiene. Every young girl or woman should shower every day, if possible, with warm water. Hygiene is very important at all times but especially during this period because various forms of bacteria gather in the passage from which the blood flows, often causing a severe odor of the menstrual blood. Combining this with the emission of oils from the sebaceous glands, which are usually more active during this period, the odor can increase greatly.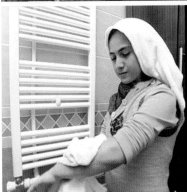

In addition to this, there are also changes in the skin and body odors of women during this period. If hygiene is ignored during this period, the odors can sometimes become very offensive to others. Therefore personal hygiene is very important during the menstrual period, and young girls in particular should make personal hygiene a regular habit from an early age to enable them to live a healthy life.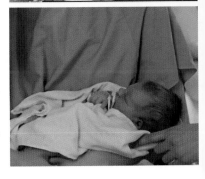

Nifas (Post-Childbirth Bleeding)

What is nifas?

Nifas is the blood discharged from the woman's body after childbirth. *Nifas* is also known as the postnatal period. The minimum duration of the discharge of blood during the *nifas*, or postnatal period, is uncertain because it can vary greatly according to every individual. However, the maximum duration of *nifas* is forty days. The bleeding that continues after forty days is not classified as postnatal bleeding but is considered as abnormal bleeding or bleeding due to illness. The duration of the postnatal period is defined when the bleeding ends within the forty day duration following childbirth.

What is prohibited in Islam during the menstrual and post-childbirth periods?

During the menstrual and postnatal periods women are classified as ritually impure and, therefore, are neither permitted nor obliged to perform specific acts of worship during this period. The forms of worship women are exempted from and are not permitted to perform during the menstrual and postnatal periods are:

❏   **Praying**

During the menstrual and postnatal periods, a woman cannot pray and is not expected to make up the missed prayers at a later date. In every aspect, Islam is the religion of convenience, and this principle of convenience is evident in the rulings and guidelines regarding the prayers of women during both the menstrual and the postnatal periods. The menstrual cycle occurs every month; thus if performing the missed prayers later had been made compulsory, this would naturally entail great difficulty upon the individual. The Prophet explained this in one of the hadith: "Abandon the prayer when your menses begins, and when it ends, perform *ghusl* (bathing) and then pray."

❑ Fasting

Women are exempt from fasting during the menstrual and postnatal periods. But unlike the prayers, it is compulsory for women to perform the fasts they were unable to observe at a later date. Fasting is not a form of worship performed continuously on a daily basis like the prayer; therefore, compensating for the fasts at a later date does not impose a burden or difficulty on the individual. Those who were unable to fast on certain days during the month of Ramadan can observe these fasts on individual days at a later date.

On the exemption of performing the prayers and the obligation of compensating for the fasts missed during these specific periods Aisha, the dear wife of the Prophet related: "When any of us got our menses or bleeding after childbirth, the Prophet ordered us to make up for the missed fasts. He never ordered us to make up the missed prayers."

❑ Handling the Qur'ân

It is not permissible for women during their menstrual and post-childbirth bleeding to handle the Qur'ân directly, but they may hold it with a clean cloth or another item.

❑ Reading the Qur'ân

During menstrual and post-childbirth bleeding, women are not permitted to read the Qur'ân themselves; however, they may listen to the recitation of the Qur'ân. They may recite the verses of supplication (*du'â'*); for example, "Rabbanâ âtinâ," with the intention of supplicating to God. They may recite any of the verses which bear meaning of supplication, and they may recite the prayers of praise and glorification. It is permissible for a woman mention the name of God and to recite words bearing remembrance of the Creator during the menstrual and postnatal periods; for example, *Subhân Allâh*, *Lâ ilâha illallâh*, and *Alhamdulillâh*. They may submit any kind of supplication and, therefore, not be deprived of remembering and supplicating to their Creator.

❐   **Performing Tawaf (Circumambulating) around the Ka'bah**

During menstrual and post-childbirth bleeding, women are not permitted to enter mosques or to perform *tawaf* around the Ka'bah. The Prophet said: "It is not permissible for those in a state of menstruation or major impurity (after marital relations or seminal emission) to enter the mosque."

Istihâdha (Bleeding due to Illness)

Istihâdha is the name given to the discharge of blood from the womb that is not due to menstrual or post-childbirth bleeding. This blood is different from that of *haydh* and *nifas*. This blood flows directly from the veins, and is therefore thin and odorless like the blood that flows from the nose during a nosebleed or from any other organ of the body. This type of bleeding is usually due to an illness or abnormality in the womb. Therefore, this condition is considered as an ailment.

The discharge of blood which lasts for less than three days or exceeds ten days is classified as abnormal, non-menstrual bleeding. The post-childbirth bleeding which lasts for more than forty days is also abnormal bleeding, and the discharge of blood from girls less than nine or women over fifty five years old is regarded as the loss of blood due to an illness or abnormal condition. The restrictions for women during the menstrual and postnatal periods do not apply for a woman experiencing abnormal bleeding. A woman in such a condition can perform the duties of worship as usual.

THE MAIN PILLAR OF RELIGION

Daily Prayers

"The earlier part of the prescribed prayer time is the source of God's good pleasure, the middle His Mercy, and the latter part the means for His forgiveness."
Hadith

What Is the Prayer?

Why is the prayer so important?

The first condition of being a Muslim is believing in the existence and unity of God, and that Prophet Muhammad, peace and blessings be upon him, is the servant and Messenger of God. The most important command in Islam following faith is the prayer (*salâh*). Prayer is the main pillar of the religion, and an uncompromising condition of being a Muslim. Prayer is the connection between the servant and his Creator. The devoted believer stands before God, addressing His eternal compassion five times every day. During every prayer, a Muslim symbolically experiences the Prophet's union with his Creator on the *Mi'râj* (the Ascension). This is why the Prophet said: "Prayer is the Ascension of a believer (to His proximity)."

Islam is more particular regarding the establishment of the prayer than any other form of worship. For example our faith allows those journeying during Ramadan to delay the fasts and compensate for the fast on a later occasion. Muslims are commanded to give 1/40 or 2.5% of their wealth, but there is no condition of when the prescribed alms should be distributed, and there are also various other means of convenience for those obliged to give the alms. There is no ruling compelling a person to perform the pilgrimage as soon as the pilgrimage becomes compulsory. However, the subject of the prayer is totally different. In fact, to abandon a prayer a person must be on his deathbed or insane. Islam commands us to pray at all conditions, at times of war or in peace. It further tells us:

Pray at the prescribed time standing. If you are unable to do so then pray in the sitting position, if you are unable to do so then pray in the lying position, and if this is impossible, make intention to pray with your minds. If you cannot find water, then perform the tayammum (dry ablution). But certainly pray at the prescribed time.

A Special Message from the Prophet:

"Prayer Comes First"

During the last stages of the Prophet's illness and only a short time before his death Abbas, the Prophet's uncle, and Ali helped the Prophet to the prayer niche of the mosque. Those who actually witnessed the Prophet walking towards the mosque reported that he was dragging his holy feet on the ground leaving trails in the sand behind him, obviously in great pain.

The most beloved servant of God, His devoted Messenger was sent to us as guidance. The Master of the Universe, who sent His beloved Messenger as an example for mankind, did not exempt His beloved servant from the prayer just hours before his death. It was almost as if God the Almighty was looking over His servant saying, "I see your condition and your pain, but I want you to continue your prayers. You must convey to your people the importance of the prayer. Let them see that you did not abandon your prayers even in this state of affliction, so that they too will never abandon their prayers, and know that their feeble excuses regarding the establishment of the prayer will not be acceptable. Regardless of any difficulties, they must be able to say 'Prayer comes first' in every aspect of their lives."

Prayer: The Shield against all Evil

In the Qur'ân, the Sustainer of the universe bestowed the tidings, *"Establish the Prayer in conformity with its conditions. Surely, the Prayer restrains from all that is indecent and shameful, and all that is evil"* ('Ankabût 29:45). Those who pray say *Ihdinas-sirâtal-mustaqîm* ("guide us to the straight path") when they recite *Al-Fâtihah* in every *rak'ah* (unit) of the prayer, a supplication that is repeated forty times every day. Therefore, those who are fully aware of the words proclaimed during the prayer remember the covenant made to God before committing any sin, and considering the promises and words supplicated to the Creator during the prayer, they will make every effort to avoid sin. Prayers performed to perfection and with total submission prevent a person from committing sin, dishonesty, and injustice and from causing harm to others. Prayer is the shield of protection against every kind of evil.

Does praying five times daily become tiring?

The idea that prayer can be boring or tiresome because it is repeated five times daily is an excuse, a clear display of idleness and heedlessness of the human soul. A person eats food and drinks water regularly on a daily basis, but never becomes bored or tired of doing so. In fact, eating and drinking gives a person pleasure. So can a person whose soul demands spiritual satisfaction possibly grow bored or tired of praying? Prayer is the means of spiritual contentment for the human soul. Satan aims to encourage these types of negative assumptions in humans, but mainly inspires such idle conceptions in people when they initially begin to pray. Those who perform the prayer on a regular basis, and reach the spiritual abundance of the prayer, recognize the irrationality of such excuses. A human does not consist merely of flesh and bones; the soul is also an entrustment bestowed upon every human by the Creator and therefore must never be neglected.

Are worldly duties an excuse for neglecting the prayer?

Our Creator blessed us with twenty four hours of life every day we exist on earth and only expects us to spend an hour performing our daily duty of worship. The five daily prayers, together with the ritual of purification, require at the most an hour to perform. The remaining twenty three hours is more than sufficient to enable us to execute our worldly duties. If a human can allocate time for routine, and on many occasions unimportant duties, then the only logical explanation for the excuse of not being able to dedicate time for the prayer, is submission to the evil influence of Satan. If somebody offers us money or an expensive gift in return for a certain duty, without doubt we would continue that duty for days in expectation of receiving whatever we were promised. Regardless of the prospect that the person may not abide by his promise, we could work for days without becoming bored or tired of performing that duty. However the Creator, the One who never breaks His promise, guarantees us the greatest reward of all: He promises us Paradise in return for performing a duty as simple as the prayer. Therefore, not allocating just one hour of an entire twenty four hours for the prayer in return for such a reward seems somewhat illogical.

Is the prayer only compulsory when you get old?

The idea that prayer is a duty to be performed in old age is a common conception that, unfortunately, often prevents people from performing their religious duties. As we mentioned previously, the prayer is compulsory upon every Muslim, from the age of puberty, until the time of death. Age has no bearing on the compulsion of the prayer, and every missed prayer continues to be the duty, an obligation of the individual in this life and the hereafter. The only means of escaping from this obligation of the prayer that must be redeemed before death is performing every missed prayer. Death can come to any of us at any moment. There is no guarantee of living a long life, and those who neglect the prayer will go before the Creator with the heavy burden of unfulfilled duties. If we consider the fact that every single prayer neglected is a burden of debt upon every Muslim, it is clear that a Muslim who begins to pray in the later stages of life will stand before the Creator with quite a significant burden. Another point to consider is that a person may not be capable of compensating for every neglected prayer in old age, and regardless of the conception of praying in old age being unfounded, there is a great contrast between the prayers which are performed at a young age with those performed at an old age. Worship performed during the years of youth, a period in which a human battles with the worldly pleasures and inner desires to fulfill the duty of worship, is much more valuable to God. As a person reaches old age, the desires of worldly pleasures begin to fade, and a person who gradually senses death approaching feels compelled to pray mainly due to fear.

This is why the Prophet stressed in one of the hadith: "The most excellent youth is the one who thinks of death like an old person, prepares for the hereafter, and avoids drowning in blindness among the passions of youth."

When should daily prayers be performed? Why is the time for the prayer so important?

There are five obligatory prayers every day: the morning, noon, late afternoon, evening, and the night prayers. These five prayers are called the prescribed prayers. The prescribed prayers must be performed within the prescribed periods of when the time for the prayer begins and ends. Praying during the prescribed time bears great importance because this is the act of duty that pleases God the most. The greatest reward is ascribed to the prayer performed in the earlier part of the prescribed duration of time, or immediately following the call to prayer. In one of the hadith, the Prophet says: "The earlier part of the prescribed prayer time is the source of God's good pleasure, the middle His Mercy, and the latter part the means of His forgiveness."

A Muslim is not excused for the prayers not performed within the prescribed period, and prayers that are missed must be made up at the earliest possible time. When a delayed prayer is performed, the individual may be relieved of the burden of that prayer, but this does not eliminate the sin of not performing the duty of worship within the due period. The delayed prayer is by no means equal to the prayer performed within the prescribed time.

Adhân: The Call to Prayer

Adhân is the name given to the sacred words recited to inform Muslims of the prescribed prayer times five times a day. The call to the five daily prayers and the Friday prayer is a Sunnah that was highly recommended by the Prophet. The *adhân* was first recited by Bilal al-Habashî for morning prayer during the first year of the

Prophet's migration to the city of Medina. The person responsible for reciting the *adhân* is called a *muezzin*, and Bilal was the first *muezzin* of Islam.

Being an important public symbol of Islam, the *adhân* is the Muslim's invitation to the prayer, the call to stand before the Creator in worship. It is the announcement of the existence and unity of God, and the Prophethood of God's Messenger. The *adhân* is the symbol of Muslims and the Islamic faith. Thus the virtue of reciting the *adhân* is great, and the reward is plentiful. The Prophet said, "Anyone who hears a *muezzin*'s call of the *adhân* as far as it reaches, be he man or jinn, or any other creature, will testify for the *muezzin* on the Day of Judgment and ask for his forgiveness."

Where does the adhân originate from?

During the first days of Islam, the Muslims living in Mecca under the persecution and cruelty of the polytheist Quraysh had to meet and worship in secret. During this period, openly inviting the believers to the prayer was totally out of the question. But regardless of all the difficulties they faced during the initial period of their faith, there were great changes after the migration to Medina, and the Muslims were eventually free to pray and perform worship as they wished. The Masjid an-Nabawî (Prophet's Mosque) had been constructed, but there was yet no means of inviting the Muslims to the prayer. At prayer time, the Muslims called one another to the mosque with the words *as-salâh, as-salâh*! ("Come to the prayer, come to the prayer!") or *as-salâtu jami'ah*! ("Gather for the prayer!"). The Muslims realized that calling people to prayer in such a manner was insufficient. It was almost impossible for many to hear the call as they lived far away, and they were therefore unable to reach the mosque in time for prayer. Gathering the believers for the congregational prayers was a very difficult task, so they had to find a solution.

One day the Prophet called his Companions, and after explaining the difficulties they faced, he asked for their suggestions regarding a solution to the problem. The Companions presented many suggestions; some proposed ringing a bell like the Christians while others suggested blowing a horn like the Jews or lighting a fire like the Zoroastrians. But the Prophet disapproved of all of the ideas. That night 'Abdullâh ibn Zayd, one of the devoted Companions, had a dream. This is how he explained the dream:

> *A man wearing a green gown came to me while I was between sleep and wakefulness; he was standing on a wall. The man was holding a bell in his hand so I asked him, "Can I buy that bell?". The man asked, "What do you want it for?" I replied, "I will use it to call the people to the prayer." The man replied, "What if I teach you something better?" I agreed, and then the man turned towards the qiblah and recited the entire adhân. Then he repeated every word of the adhân again, but this time towards the end he added "Qad qâmatis-Salâh" ("Now the fard prayer is about to be performed"), proclaiming the iqâmah (i.e., the second call after the adhân announcing that the fard prayer is about to begin).*

Early the next morning, 'Abdullâh ibn Zayd went to the Prophet and explained his dream. The Prophet replied, "By God, this was a true dream," approving the *adhân* as the call for the prayer. Then he told 'Abdullâh to teach Bilal the exact words he heard in his dream. At prayer time, the whole of Medina echoed with the sound of Bilal's voice spreading over the horizon. 'Umar ran from his house to the Prophet as quickly as possible and in a state of excitement when he heard the call to prayer. When he heard about 'Abdullâh's dream, 'Umar said: "O Messenger of God! I swear by the One who sent you with the religion of truth, I saw exactly the same dream too."

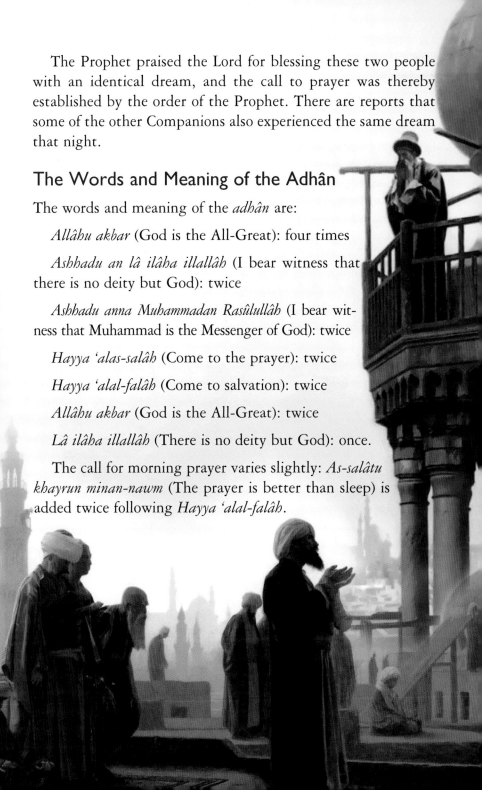

The Prophet praised the Lord for blessing these two people with an identical dream, and the call to prayer was thereby established by the order of the Prophet. There are reports that some of the other Companions also experienced the same dream that night.

The Words and Meaning of the Adhân

The words and meaning of the *adhân* are:

Allâhu akbar (God is the All-Great): four times

Ashhadu an lâ ilâha illallâh (I bear witness that there is no deity but God): twice

Ashhadu anna Muhammadan Rasûlullâh (I bear witness that Muhammad is the Messenger of God): twice

Hayya 'alas-salâh (Come to the prayer): twice

Hayya 'alal-falâh (Come to salvation): twice

Allâhu akbar (God is the All-Great): twice

Lâ ilâha illallâh (There is no deity but God): once.

The call for morning prayer varies slightly: *As-salâtu khayrun minan-nawm* (The prayer is better than sleep) is added twice following *Hayya 'alal-falâh*.

The Supplication Recited after the Adhân

The Prophet explained the importance of listening as the *adhân* is recited, and he also advised us to recite certain supplications during and after the call of *adhân*. He told us in one of the hadith:

> *When you hear the adhân you should repeat the exact words as after the muezzin except when you hear "Hayya 'alas-salâh," you should say "Lâ hawla walâ quwwata illâ billâh" ("There is no might and no power save with God"). And when the muezzin says "Hayya 'alal-falâh," you should say "Mâ shâ Allâhu kâna wa mâ lam yasha' lam yakun" ("That which God wills occurs, that which He does not desire will not occur") and then continue to recite the same words of the muezzin. When the adhân is completed recite this supplication: "Allâhumma Rabba hâdhihid-da'watit-tâmmah, was-salâtil-qâimah; âti sayyidanâ Muhammadanil-wasîlata wal-fadîlah wad-darajatal-âliyah, wab'athhu Maqâman-Mahmûdanil-ladhî wa'adtahu; innaka lâ tuhliful-mîâd," (which means: "O God, Lord of this perfect call and established prayer. Bestow upon our Master Muhammad the right of intercession and the rank above the rest of creation, and raise him to the honored station You have promised him. Verily, You never fail in Your promise").*

The Prophet then said, "Whoever does as such (i.e. repeats the words of the *muezzin* and recites these supplications) will be assured of my intercession on the Day of Judgment."

Respecting the Call to Prayer

There is no specific regulation of how we should listen to the *adhân*; more important is hearing, understanding, and respecting the call to prayer. A person may remain silent, speak, or read accordingly under the

The Tomb of Bilal al-Habashi

condition there is no bearing of disrespect in what is being said or done at the time. There is no objection of being occupied while the *adhân* is being called. God the Almighty judges the intention of a human, and religion does not prevent a person from performing the daily requirements or demands.

However, if we are listening to music it is better to turn the music off until the call to prayer ends. Laughing aloud or continuing to shout or speak loud in conversation during the *adhân* is considered disrespectful. In addition to this, whenever possible a person should avoid entering the toilet when *adhân* is being called.

The Iqâmah before the Fard Prayers

The *iqâmah* is the words of the *adhân* recited before the *fard* prayers. The *adhân* is called when the time of the prescribed prayer begins, whereas *iqâmah* is recited immediately before the *fard* prayers are performed. The words of the *iqâmah* are the same as the *adhân*; the only difference is that "Qad qâmati's-salâh" ("Now the prayer is about to begin") is recited twice following "Hayya 'alal-falâh." The *iqâmah* is not recited like the *adhân* in a long melodic manner. It is, rather, recited more quickly and in a normal tone of voice. A person who performs the prayer alone may recite both the *adhân* and the *iqâmah*, or just the *iqâmah*. Women are not required to say *iqâmah*. Also, though it is not compulsory for men to recite the *iqâmah* if the individual is in a hurry, he will be rewarded for performing a sunnah of the Prophet if he does.

The Conditions of Prayer

How many acts are compulsory for prayer?

There are twelve compulsory conditions of performing the prayer, six of which are prior to the prayer, and six during the prayer. The six acts that are compulsory prior to the prayer are the actions necessary to perform worship. These are called the "Conditions of

Prayer." The six obligatory acts during prayer are the actions that must be included in the prayer for the prayer to be valid, and these are referred to as the "*Rukn*s, or Elements, of Prayer."

What are the conditions prior to prayer?

These are the conditions that must be performed before prayer:

1. Purification from the *hadath* (ritual impurities)
2. Purification from the *najâsah* (material impurities)
3. *Satr al-'awrah*
4. *Istiqbâl al-qiblah*
5. *Al-waqt*
6. *Niyyah*

What is purification from the *hadath* (ritual impurities)?

Before the prayer, a person must be purified of ritual impurities known as *hadath*, which prevents the person from performing worship. This is done by performing ablution before the prayer or by performing *ghusl* (bathing) when in a state of major impurity, such as seminal emission after marital relations and wet dreams.

What is purification from the *najâsah* (material impurities)?

Najâsah is the word given to material impurities. Before praying, a person's clothing, body, and the area for prayer must be purified from any substance that is classified as impure. The impurities that invalidate the prayer were mentioned in the previous chapter on *tahârah*.

However, it is to be noted here that one must ensure the cleanliness of underwear and private parts after the call of nature and must be careful about letting not even a drop of urine splash on their body or garments. Cleaning the private parts with water and using toilet paper to dry the private parts is certainly the best way for a thorough cleansing.

In addition, one must take great care that the drops of urine have come to an end before making ablution. In particular, men must ensure that there are no drops of urine before making the ablution, for the emission of any urine after the ablution, no matter how small the amount, invalidates the ablution. Therefore, men should be very sensitive about this matter. In order to be sure men can adopt habits that are recommended, such as coughing while waiting for the release of urine to cease or taking a brisk walk after relieving themselves.

What is satr al-'awrah?

Satr al-'awrah is covering the parts of the body not permitted to be seen by others.

These are the areas of the bodies of both men and women prohibited to be seen by other people. During the prayer, a man must cover at the least from his navel to below the kneecaps, whereas a woman must cover her entire body, with the exception of her hands and face.

In addition to this, we must also consider the fact that during the prayer, we stand before our Creator; therefore, it is necessary to dress accordingly when we pray. A person should avoid wearing tight clothing while praying, and is not permitted to pray while wearing thin clothing through which the color of the skin is apparent.

What is istiqbâl al-qiblah?

The direction to be faced during the prayers (*qiblah*) is the Ka'bah, which is in the city of Mecca. *Istiqbâl al-qiblah* means literally turning towards the Ka'bah to perform the prayer. The *qiblah* does not only consist of the structure of the Ka'bah.

According to the Islamic faith, the *qiblah* is a pillar of light rising above the Ka'bah into the highest Heaven, and beneath the Ka'bah to the very center of the earth. So whether we are on a plane or beneath the grounds surface, we can turn towards this pillar of light that is in alignment with the Ka'bah and pray. If we do not know the direction of the *qiblah*, the best thing to do is ask somebody else if possible. If there is no possible means of learning the direction of the *qiblah*, then we must try to determine the direction using our own initiative, the direction that our hearts believe to be correct. In which case, if we do pray in the wrong direction by mistake, our prayers will still be valid. If we realize that we prayed in the wrong direction by mistake, or learn the course of the *qiblah* after praying, we are not obliged to repeat the prayer. However, if we pray without inquiring or trying to determine the right direction by our own instincts, then we must perform the prayer again.

What is al-waqt?

Every prayer has a prescribed time during which the prayer must be prayed. Performing the five daily prayers on time is an obligation upon every Muslim. This is called *al-waqt*, "the prescribed time." It is not permissible to pray before the prescribed time begins, and a prayer performed after the prescribed time ends is not classified as fulfilling our duty of performing the prescribed prayer. This is compensating for the prayer we missed.

What is niyyah?

The *niyyah*, or intention for the prayer, is the desire of praying for the sake of God and acknowledging which prayer is to be performed. For instance, affirming "O Lord! I intend to pray the *fard* of the noon prayer for Your pleasure" in the heart is sufficient for fulfilling the condition of the intention for prayer. There is no requirement of specifying the number of *rak'ah*s (units) of the prayer. When praying in congregation the imam and those following him must have the intention of doing so. The intention for praying a congregational prayer should be: "I comply with the imam" asserting that the individual intends to conform to the imam during the prayer. And the imam's intention should be words to the effect of: "I intend to lead the prayer of those who comply with me."

What are the obligatory acts during the prayer?

The obligatory (*fard*) acts during the prayer are:

1. *Takbîratul-iftitah*
2. *Qiyâm*
3. *Qirâ'ah*
4. *Rukû'*
5. *Sajdah*
6. *Qa'dah al-âkhirah*

What is Takbîratul-iftitah?

Takbîratul-iftitah, or the opening *takbîr*,[2] is proclaiming God's name by reciting "Allâhu akbar" at the beginning of the prayer. The intention for the prayer must be made before the opening *takbîr* is pronounced, and the *takbîr* must be pronounced while in the standing position, looking at the point where one puts his forehead during prostration. While reciting the *takbîr*, one raises the hands with the palms facing the *qiblah*, according to the Hanafis, to the ears, with the thumbs touching the earlobes (or in front of the chest for women). In addition to this, a person should not eat, drink, speak or perform any action of disrespect between the intention and *takbîr* of the prayer.

2   This opening *takbîr* is also called the *takbîratul-ihrâm* (*takbîr* of consecration). The person praying enters into the consecrated state of prayer after the recitation of this formula of consecration, and thus things which are not part of the prayer become forbidden for the person who gets into this consecrated state of prayer.

What is qiyâm?

Qiyâm means standing upright during the prayer. It is compulsory to perform the obligatory prayers in the standing position. However, those who are unable to pray standing up may perform the prayer in the sitting position. A person who begins the prayer standing but during the prayer feels too weak to pray in the standing position may continue the prayer in the sitting position.

What is qirâ'ah?

During the prayer, it is compulsory to recite a portion of the Qur'ân–this is called *qirâ'ah*. It is compulsory to recite three short or one equally long verse of the Qur'ân while standing during the prayer. During the congregational prayers, the imam recites verses of the Qur'ân, and those who comply with the imam for the prayer do not recite the Qur'ân themselves but listen to the imam's recitation.

What is rukû'?

Rukû' is bowing during the prayer to the extent that the head and back are straight in alignment towards the *qiblah* while holding the kneecaps with the fingers spread out. According to the Hanafis, women are not required to bow fully during prayer. They bow over slightly and do not hold the knees during the *rukû'* but simply place both hands on the knees.

What is sajdah?

Sajdah is prostrating by placing the nose, forehead, hands, knees, and feet on the ground. During prayer, we prostrate by firstly placing both knees, then both hands together with the head on the ground. It is compulsory to perform the prostration twice during every *rak'ah* (unit) of the prayer. It is not advisable to prostrate on a soft object that prevents the individual from sensing the firmness of the ground.

Prostration is the most important element of the prayer; it is the ultimate display of a person's respect and submission to the Creator. Prostration is the clear expression of devotion, a believer's demonstration of servitude. This is why the Prophet said: "The closest a servant comes to God is when he prostrates."

Throught the prayer the eyes of the praying person should point to the spot where the forehead rests in the prostrations.

What is qa'dah al-âkhirah?

Qa'dah al-âkhirah is remaining in the seated position following the prostrations of the final *rak'ah* of the prayer for a duration sufficient to recite *at-tahiyyât*. This is called the last sitting. In the Hanafi School, during *qa'dah al-âkhirah*, or the last sit-

ting, men sit in the kneeling position with the outer side of the left foot and leg on the ground and the right foot and toes pointing downwards, whereas women sit on the left hip and leg, with both legs facing towards the right. Altering the methods of the sitting position due to health or disability reasons is permissible.

The Wâjib (Necessary) Acts of Prayer

In addition to the obligatory acts of prayer, there are also *wâjib* (necessary) elements of the prayer. The *wâjib* acts of prayer are:

1. Pronouncing "Allâhu akbar"—the *takbîratul-iftitah*.

2. Reciting *Al-Fâtihah* in every unit of the prayer.

3. Reciting verses of the Qur'ân after *Al-Fâtihah*.

4. In addition to the forehead, also placing the nose on the ground during prostration.

5. After the second unit of a prayer consisting of three or four units, remaining in the sitting position for a period sufficient to recite *at-tahiyyât*, then rising to the standing position immediately and continuing the third unit of the prayer.

6. Reciting *at-tahiyyât* during both of the sitting positions of the prayer.

7. Reciting the *qunût* supplications during the *witr* prayers.

8. Not hurrying the prayer and fulfilling every element of the prayer to perfection.

9. Giving *salâm* (greetings) at the end of the prayer.

10. Performing *sujûdus-sahw* due to a mistake during prayer.

What is sujûdus-sahw (prostrations of forgetfulness)?

Sujûdus-sahw is the prostrations performed at the end of a prayer with the intention of compensating for an omission or mistake performed during the prayer. However, performing the *sujûdus-*

sahw is not sufficient if one or more of the *fard*, or obligatory, acts are omitted during the prayer. In such a case, the prayer is considered invalid and must be repeated. One must perform the prostrations of forgetfulness if one of the obligatory acts of prayer is delayed, or a *wâjib* element of the prayer is omitted due to forgetfulness, such as leaving out the first sitting (*tashahhud*) at the end of the first two units of the prayer and standing up for the third *rak'ah* (unit) of the prayer.

The individual who unintentionally makes a mistake during the prayer gives *salâm* in the last sitting of the prayer after reciting *at-tahiyyât* to the left and the right, immediately pronounces "Allâhu akbar," and then performs prostration twice.

Following the two prostrations, the individual recites *at-tahiyyât* for the second time and then continues to recite the supplications and gives *salâm* as usual. By performing the prostrations and recitations as prescribed, the prostration of forgetfulness is complete. If the imam makes a mistake during the congregational prayers, *salâm* is given towards the right side only, and then the *sujûdus-sahw* must be performed. The reason for abstaining from giving *salâm* to the left is to prevent the congregation from ending the prayer until the *sujûdus-sahw* has been performed. In which case, the entire congregation is under obligation to comply and perform the prostrations of forgetfulness with the imam.

The *sujûdus-sahw* is a *wâjib* act of prayer, and unintentionally omitting a *wâjib* act does not invalidate prayer, so if the prostration of forgetfulness is not performed unintentionally, the prayer is still valid.

The Sunnah Acts of Prayer

As in any form of worship, the prayers also consist of sunnah acts. Complying with the Sunnah is clear evidence of affection for Prophet Muhammad, the Messenger of God. Although abandoning a Sunnah does not invalidate the prayer, frequently abandoning the Prophet's traditions due to mere laziness could lead to the deprivation of his intercession in the hereafter.

The principle sunnah acts of the prayer are:

1. Reciting the *adhân* and *iqâmah* for the five prescribed prayers, and the Friday prayers.

2. Men raising the hands to the ears and women to shoulder level while pronouncing the opening *takbîr* of the prayer.

3. Placing both hands below the navel for men with the right hand grasping the left one at the wrist, and placing both hands on the chest for women.

4. Before the recitation of *Al-Fâtihah*, reciting the supplication of *Subhânaka* and *A'ûdhu-Basmala* after placing the hands on the navel or chest. (The Hanafis recite the opening supplication of *Subhânaka*, but one can recite another supplication that the Prophet used to begin his prayers).

5. Saying "Amîn" when hearing or reciting *Al-Fâtihah* during the prayer.

6. Saying "Allâhu akbar" while going into the bowing position.

7. Saying "Subhâna Rabbiyal-'Azîm" ("All-Glorious is my Lord, the Mighty") at least three times while in the bowing position.

8. Saying "Subhâna Rabbiyal-A'lâ" ("All-Glorious is my Lord, the Most High") at least three times while in the prostrating position.

9. Saying "Sami'allâhu liman hamidah" ("God hears him who praises Him") while rising from the bowing position, and "Rabbanâ lakal-hamd" (Our Lord, to You is all praise") when reaching the standing position.

10. Holding the knees with fingers spread out while bowing, or for women, placing both hands on the knees.

11. Not bending the knees while bowing, facing the ground, and keeping the head and back parallel to the ground. Women may bend their legs and bow arching their backs slightly.

12. When going to prostration, placing the knees on the ground, followed by the hands, and then the face.

13. When rising from prostration, first lifting the face from the ground, followed by the hands, and then the knees.

14. Saying "Allâhu akbar" when going into and rising from prostration.

15. Placing both hands on the front of the thighs facing the *qiblah* between the two prostrations.

16. While in the sitting position, men must sit in the kneeling position with the outer side of the left leg and foot on the ground and the right foot straight with the heel pointing up and the toes downwards. Women sit on the left hip with both legs directed towards the right.

17. Reciting the Salât 'alan-Nabî (i.e., supplications *Allâhumma salli* and *Allâhumma bârik*) after *at-tahiyyât* in the last sitting.

18. Giving greetings towards the right shoulder first by saying "As-salâmu 'alaykum wa rahmatullâh," and then repeating the greetings towards the left shoulder.

19. Establishing a *sutra* when praying in an open area, or where there is the possibility of people passing. *Sutra* is an object placed in front of the individual praying as a barrier between him and passers-by so that people will not come between him and the *qiblah*.

Things That Invalidate Prayer

1. Abandoning one of the *fard* acts of the prayer with no valid excuse.

2. Talking during the prayer.

3. Eating or drinking during the prayer.

4. Laughing aloud.

5. Raising both of the feet from the ground when performing the prostration.

6. Turning the chest away from the direction of the *qiblah*.

7. Performing an act inconsistent with the prayer or actions which may lead others to assume you are not praying.

8. Greeting or accepting the greetings of others during the prayer.

9. Crying aloud due to worldly difficulties and afflictions during the prayer. However, crying due to the fear of the Divine punishment in the hereafter or previous sins does not invalidate prayer.

10. If the sun rises while performing the morning prayer.

11. Fainting during the prayer.

12. If ritual purity (ablution) is nullified during the prayer.

13. Reciting the Qur'ân so incorrectly that the meaning of the verse changes.

14. Scratching the body three times consecutively during one *rak'ah* (unit) of the prayer.

The Five Prescribed Prayers

The Morning (Fajr) Prayer

The morning prayer, which is performed between the break of dawn and the approach of sunrise, consists of a total of four units, two of which are Sunnah and two *fard*. The Sunnah units are performed before the *fard* prayers. Prophet Muhammad, peace and blessings be upon him, emphasized the importance of performing the Sunnah prayers at dawn. Therefore, one is allowed to pray the Sunnah units of the morning prayer even when the congregational prayer has started, provided that one has enough time to join the *fard* congregational prayer later on.

The Noon (Zuhr) Prayer

The noon prayer consists of ten units, four of which are *fard* and six Sunnah. Initially the first four Sunnahs are performed, followed by the four *fard*, and then the two last Sunnah units of the prayer.

The Afternoon ('Asr) Prayer

The afternoon prayer is a total of eight units, consisting of four Sunnah and four *fard* units. The four Sunnah are performed, which is then followed by the *fard* units of the prayer. Only the *fard* units of the afternoon prayer should be performed if there is forty five minutes or less remaining to the end of prescribed time.

The Evening (Maghrib) Prayer

The evening prayer is made up of five units, three of which are *fard* and two Sunnah. The three *fard* units are performed first, followed by the two Sunnah.

The Night ('Ishâ') Prayer

Including the three units of *witr*, the night prayer is a total of thirteen units. The first four units of Sunnah prayer are performed, followed by the four units of *fard* prayer. After the *fard* prayers, the final two Sunnah units are performed. The three units of the *witr* prayer can be performed right after the night prayer up to the break of dawn. For the convenience of the believers, however, it can be prayed after the night prayer, so that one will not miss it because of sleep.

In performing the daily prayers, it is not permissible to combine the Sunnah and *fard* prayers, each specific prayer must be completed before beginning the next prayer.

THE CHART FOR DAILY PRAYERS

TYPE OF PRAYERS	UNITS (RAK'AH)	FAJR (Morning) 2 s. + 2 f.	ZUHR (Noon) 4 s. + 4 f. + 2 s.	'ASR (Afternoon) 4 s. + 4 f.	MAGHRIB (Evening) 3 f. + 2 s.	'ISHÂ (Night) 4 s.+4 f.+2 s.+3 v.
FIRST SUNNAH	1	Subhânaka A'ûdhu-Basmala al-Fâtihah & some more verses from the Qur'ân	Subhânaka A'ûdhu-Basmala al-Fâtihah & some more verses from the Qur'ân	Subhânaka A'ûdhu-Basmala al-Fâtihah & some more verses from the Qur'ân		Subhânaka A'ûdhu-Basmala al-Fâtihah & some more verses from the Qur'ân
	2	Basmala al-Fâtihah & some more verses from the Qur'ân at-Tahiyyât Allâhumma Salli wa Bârik Rabbanâ âtinâ wa Rabbanâghfirlî	Basmala al-Fâtihah & some more verses from the Qur'ân at-Tahiyyât	Basmala al-Fâtihah & some more verses from the Qur'ân at-Tahiyyât Allâhumma Salli wa Bârik		Basmala al-Fâtihah & some more verses from the Qur'ân at-Tahiyyât Allâhumma Salli wa Bârik
	3		Basmala al-Fâtihah & some more verses from the Qur'ân	Subhânaka A'ûdhu-Basmala al-Fâtihah & some more verses from the Qur'ân		Subhânaka A'ûdhu-Basmala al-Fâtihah & some more verses from the Qur'ân
	4		Basmala al-Fâtihah & some more verses from the Qur'ân at-Tahiyyât Allâhumma Salli wa Bârik Rabbanâ âtinâ wa Rabbanâghfirlî	Basmala al-Fâtihah & some more verses from the Qur'ân at-Tahiyyât Allâhumma Salli wa Bârik Rabbanâ âtinâ wa Rabbanâghfirlî		Basmala al-Fâtihah & some more verses from the Qur'ân at-Tahiyyât Allâhumma Salli wa Bârik Rabbanâ âtinâ wa Rabbanâghfirlî
FARD	1	Subhânaka A'ûdhu-Basmala al-Fâtihah & some more verses from the Qur'ân	Subhânaka A'ûdhu-Basmala al-Fâtihah & some more verses from the Qur'ân	Subhânaka A'ûdhu-Basmala al-Fâtihah & some more verses from the Qur'ân	Subhânaka A'ûdhu-Basmala al-Fâtihah & some more verses from the Qur'ân	Subhânaka A'ûdhu-Basmala al-Fâtihah & some more verses from the Qur'ân
	2	Basmala al-Fâtihah & some more verses from the Qur'ân at-Tahiyyât Allâhumma Salli wa Bârik Rabbanâ âtinâ wa Rabbanâghfirlî	Basmala al-Fâtihah & some more verses from the Qur'ân at-Tahiyyât	Basmala al-Fâtihah & some more verses from the Qur'ân at-Tahiyyât	Basmala al-Fâtihah & some more verses from the Qur'ân at-Tahiyyât	Basmala al-Fâtihah & some more verses from the Qur'ân at-Tahiyyât
	3		Basmala al-Fâtihah	Basmala al-Fâtihah	Basmala al-Fâtihah at-Tahiyyât Allâhumma Salli wa Bârik Rabbanâ âtinâ wa Rabbanâghfirlî	Basmala al-Fâtihah
	4		Basmala al-Fâtihah at-Tahiyyât Allâhumma Salli wa Bârik Rabbanâ âtinâ wa Rabbanâghfirlî	Basmala al-Fâtihah at-Tahiyyât Allâhumma Salli wa Bârik Rabbanâ âtinâ wa Rabbanâghfirlî		Basmala al-Fâtihah at-Tahiyyât Allâhumma Salli wa Bârik Rabbanâ âtinâ wa Rabbanâghfirlî

TYPE OF PRAYERS	UNITS (RAK'AH)	FAJR (Morning)	ZUHR (Noon)	'ASR (Afternoon)	MAGHRIB (Evening)	'ISHÂ' (Night)
		2 s. + 2 f.	4 s. + 4 f. + 2 s.	4 s. + 4 f.	3 f. + 2 s.	4 s.+4 f.+2 s.+3 v.
SECOND SUNNAH	**1**		Subhânaka A'ûdhu-Basmala al-Fâtihah & some more verses from the Qur'ân		Subhânaka A'ûdhu-Basmala al-Fâtihah & some more verses from the Qur'ân	Subhânaka A'ûdhu-Basmala al-Fâtihah & some more verses from the Qur'ân
SECOND SUNNAH	**2**		Basmala al-Fâtihah & some more verses from the Qur'ân at-Tahiyyât Allâhumma Salli wa Bârik Rabbanâ âtinâ wa Rabbanâghfirlî		Basmala al-Fâtihah & some more verses from the Qur'ân at-Tahiyyât Allâhumma Salli wa Bârik Rabbanâ âtinâ wa Rabbanâghfirlî	Basmala al-Fâtihah & some more verses from the Qur'ân at-Tahiyyât Allâhumma Salli wa Bârik Rabbanâ âtinâ wa Rabbanâghfirlî
WITR	**1**					Subhânaka A'ûdhu-Basmala al-Fâtihah & some more verses from the Qur'ân
WITR	**2**					Basmala al-Fâtihah & some more verses from the Qur'ân at-Tahiyyât
WITR	**3**					Basmala al-Fâtihah & some more verses from the Qur'ân Allâhu Akbar Qunût Prayers at-Tahiyyât Allâhumma Salli wa Bârik Rabbanâ âtinâ wa Rabbanâghfirlî

The following prayers are performed identically:

* Sunnah of Morning (*Fajr*) - second sunnah of Noon (*Zuhr*) - sunnah of Evening (*Maghrib*) - second sunnah of Night (*'Ishâ'*)
* Sunnah of Afternoon (*'Asr*) - first sunnah of Night (*'Ishâ'*)

S: Sunnah
F: Fard
W: Witr

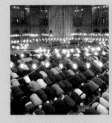

How to Perform
the Prayers

Each prayer is composed of a number of units (*rak'ah*s). Once you have learned how to perform a two-unit prayer, you will be able to perform any prayer consisting of two, three, or four units.

How to Perform the Sunnah Units of the Morning Prayer

Initially, you make the intention for the prayer in your heart: "I intend to perform the Sunnah of the morning prayer for the sake of God."

The prayer begins with the opening *takbîr*. Raise your hands, palms facing the *qiblah*, and recite "Allâhu Akbar." According to the Hanafis, men raise their hands up to the ears, with their thumbs touching the earlobes. Women raise their hands up to the shoulders, placing them in front of their chest, with the palms facing the *qiblah*.

Following the opening *takbîr*, men should place their hands just below the navel with the right hand holding onto the left one at the wrist. Women place both hands on the chest, the right hand on top of the left one.

After placing your hands in the appropriate place, recite *Subhânaka* (or any other supplication which the Prophet used to recite in his prayers.) Following this opening supplication, recite *A'ûdhu-Basmala* and then *Sûrah al-Fâtihah*. Say "Âmîn" quietly or loudly when reciting *Sûrah al-Fâtihah*. Then recite another sûrah or passage from the Qur'ân (at least three short ones or one equally long verse of the Qur'ân).

Then bow down saying "Allâhu Akbar." Recite "Subhâna Rabbiyal 'Azîm" at least three times in the bowing position (*rukû'*).

Say "Sami'allâhu liman hamidah" while rising from the bowing position, and "Rabbanâ lakal-hamd" when fully upright (i.e. after reaching the standing position).

Then say "Allâhu Akbar" while going into prostration. Recite "Subhâna Rabbiyal-A'lâ" at least three times while in the prostration position.

Then say "Allâhu Akbar" when rising from the prostration and sit upright for a moment with your knees bent and palms resting on them.

Prostrate again saying "Allâhu Akbar" and recite "Subhâna Rabbiyal-A'lâ" at least three times while in the prostration position. Then stand up from the prostration position saying "Allâhu Akbar." This completes one rak'ah, or unit, of the prayer.

The second rak'ah, or unit, of the prayer is performed in the same manner as the first rak'ah above, except that you only recite "Bismillâhir-Rahmânir-Rahîm" without reciting the opening prayer of Subhânaka.

Following the prostrations of the second rak'ah (unit) of the prayer, remain seated and recite the prayers of at-tahiyyât, Salât alan Nabî (i.e., Allâhumma Salli and Allâhumma Bârik) as well as Rabbâna Âtinâ and Rabbanâghfirlî while in the sitting position. Then give salâms (peace greetings), saying "as-salâmu 'alaykum wa rahmatullâh" while turning your head to the right and left (both times). When you give salâms, turn your head first to the right and then the left, with the eyes looking down at the shoulder. This completes the two-Sunnah unit of the morning prayer.

After completing the two fard-units of the morning prayer in the same way, then recite the *tasbihâtus-salâh* as a supplement of prayer in remembrance of God. First recite *A'ûdhu-Basmala* and then *Âyatul Kursî.* Then recite the *tasbihât*, or words, of glorification ("Subhân Allâh"), of praise ("al-hamdulillah"), and of exaltation ("Allâhu Akbar"), 33 times each.

Finally, you make *du'â's.* You can pray to God, ask for forgiveness and mercy from Him, and offer greetings to the Prophet. You can pray in your own language and in your own words to your heart's content.

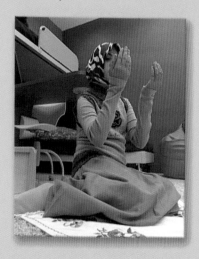

How to Perform the Fard Units of the Morning Prayer

The *fard* units are performed in the same manner as the Sunnah units of the morning prayer, the only difference being the intention for prayer. Before beginning the *fard* units of the morning prayer, the individual must make the intention, "I intend to perform the *fard* of the morning prayer for the sake of God" in the heart. In addition to this, the *iqâmah* is also recited before beginning the *fard* prayer. It is Sunnah for men to recite the *iqâmah* before performing the *fard* units of every prayer.

How to Perform the Other Prayers

All of the Sunnah prayers consisting of two units are performed in the same manner as the Sunnah of the morning prayers; the only difference is the intention for prayer. The individual must have the intention of performing that specific prayer. If the Sunnah prayers consist of four units, *at-tahiyyât* is recited during the first sitting after the first two units of the prayer, and the individual immediately rises to the standing position for the third unit of the prayer. In the third and fourth units of the Sunnah prayers only *Basmala* is pronounced before the recitation of *Al-Fâtihah*.

It is to be noted that in the first sitting of the Sunnah units of the afternoon and the first Sunnahs of the night prayer, the supplications *Allâhumma salli* and *Allâhumma bârik* are recited after the recitation of *at-tahiyyât*, and when standing for the third unit of these two prayers, reciting Subhânaka and *A'ûdhu-Basmala* is necessary, whereas in the fourth unit of the prayer only *Basmala* is pronounced before reciting *Al-Fâtihah*.

After expressing the intention of performing a specific prayer, all of the *fard* prayers are executed in the same way as the *fard* units of the morning prayer. After reciting *Al-Fâtihah* in the third and fourth units of the *fard* prayers of the noon, afternoon and night prayers and the third unit of the evening prayers no other verses of the Qur'ân are recited.

Witr Prayer

◆ The *witr* prayer is a *wâjib* act of worship that consists of three units. First, the individual defines the intention for prayer: "I intend to perform the *witr* prayers for the sake of God."

◆ The first two units are performed in the same way as the Sunnah of the morning prayer.

◆ On completion of the prostrations following the second unit the individual remains seated, and following the recitation of *at-tahiyyât*, he or she rises to the standing position and recites *Al-Fâtihah* followed by another *sûrah* or Qur'anic verses, after which men raise their hands to ear level and women chest level to pronounce the *takbîr*.

◆ The hands are then placed on the navel or chest again, and the *Qunût* supplications are recited (The *Qunût* supplications are a *wâjib* act of the prayer).

◆ After the recitation of the *Qunût* supplications, the individual bows and performs the prostrations as usual.

◆ In the last sitting of the prayer following the prostrations, the usual supplications are recited, and then greetings are given to the right and left, therefore completing the prayer.

What are the tasbihâtus-salâh (glorifications recited after the prayer)?

Various *tasbihât* (words of glorification repeated in a set number of times) and *du'a*s (prayers and supplications) are recited after worship as a supplement of prayer and in remembrance of God. The Prophet recited these *tasbihât* and *du'â*'s after every prayer and advised all Muslims to practice this on a regular basis. The manner of performing *tasbihât* after the prayer is:

• Reciting "Allâhumma antas-Salâmu wa minkas-Salâm. Tabarakta yâ Dhal-Jalâli wal-Ikrâm" after giving *salâm* on completion of the *fard* prayers. The meaning of this supplication is as follows: "O God, You are Peace, and from You is peace. You are the All-Blessed and One bestowing blessings, O One of Majesty and Munificence."

• If there is no Sunnah units after the *fard* prayers, "Allâhumma salli 'alâ Sayidinâ Muhammad" should be recited after the above supplication.

• This is followed by "Subhânallâhi wal-hamdu lillâhi wa lâ ilâha illallâhu wallâhu akbar. Wa lâ hawla wa lâ quwwata illâ billâhil 'azîm" (Glory be to God and all praise to God, there is no deity other than God, God is the All-Great. None has the majesty and none has power to sustain except God.) This is followed by the *A'ûdhu-Basmala* and the recitation of *Âyatul-Kursî* ("the Verse of the Throne" in Sûrah al-Baqarah 2:255).

• Subsequently the following words of glorification, praise and exaltation are each recited thirty three times in the following order: "Subhân Allâh," "alhamdulillâh," and "Allâhu akbar".

Subhân Allâh bears the meanings "Glory be to God, He who is free from all fault." *Alhamdulillâh* means "Praise is for God alone. Only God is worthy of praise and gratitude," and *Allâhu akbar* means "God is the All-Great."

• Followed by "Lâ ilâha illallâhu wahdahû lâ sharîka lah. Lahul mulku wa lahul hamdu wa huwa 'alâ kulli shay'in qadîr" which is followed by a supplication of prayer.

The meaning of the above supplication is: "There is none worthy of worship but God, He is One and has no partner. His is the kingdom (universe), only He is worthy of all praise. God has power over all things."

Congregational Prayers

The *fard* prayers can be performed either alone or in congregation. Performing the prayers in congregation is emphasized by the Prophet, and it is not difficult to form a congregation for the prayer as two people are sufficient to form a congregation—one as the imam and the other the congregation. Therefore, if a person is praying, for instance, the second unit of the first Sunnah of the noon prayer alone and finds some people starting their *fard* prayer in congregation, he should abandon his prayer by giving *salâm* at the end of the second unit of his prayer and join the congregation.

According to the Hanafis, it is a strong Sunnah for men to perform the five daily prayers in congregation, and *fard* to per-

form the Friday prayers in a congregational prayer. In addition, Muslim women should dress modestly while going out or to the mosque; therefore, she should wear neither transparent, tight-fitting clothing nor perfumes while praying in the mosque.

Is the reward greater for performing congregational prayers?

Performing the prayers in congregation bears great importance in our religion. Although the congregational prayers were not pre-scribed an obligatory duty by God, the Prophet emphasized that the reward for praying among a community is twenty seven times greater than the reward for praying alone. In one of the hadith the Prophet said: "Whoever attends the mosque for prayer will be for-given one sin for each step taken, and his degree will be raised one level," and in another hadith: "One who performs the night prayer in congregation is as if he has prayed for half of the night. And one who performs the morning prayer in congregation as well is as if he has prayed the whole night."

The prayer performed in congregation encourages brother-hood and charity, arouses our emotions of respecting and caring for each other, and helps us to protect our unity and solidarity as a community.

How to Perform the Congregational Prayers

Those who comply with the imam for the congregational prayer must make the intention for both the prayer and com-pliance with the imam. After the imam pronounces the open-ing *takbîr*, the congregation also performs the *takbîr*, and then recites *Subhânaka*. According to the Hanafis, the congregation does not recite *Al-Fâtihah* or any other verses of the Qur'ân with the imam. Followers of various Islamic schools should, therefore, take into consideration the difference of preferences regarding it. As the imam bows, those performing the prayer also bow down and recite "Subhâna Rabbiyal-'Azîm" ("All-Glorious is my Lord, the Mighty") (at least) three times. When the imam rises from the bowing position and says, "Sami'allâhu liman hamidah," those praying behind him silently say, "Rabbanâ lakal-hamd" ("Our Lord, to You is all praise",) and then follow the imam to prostration and recite "Subhâna Rabbiyal-A'lâ" ("All-Glorious is my Lord, the Most High") (at least) three times. Only *at-tahiyyât* is recited in the first sitting of a three or four unit prayer, and in the last sitting *at-tahiyyât*, the two supplications of the *Salât 'alan Nabî* ("Blessings for the Prophet") and then the usual supplications recited during the last sitting. Finally, those praying bestow *salâm* ("greetings") towards the right and the left together with the imam, thus completing prayer.

What should a latecomer do if the prayer has already begun?

First of all, the latecomer should not run or hasten to join the congregation but should walk with ease and dignity, and he should join the existing rows of congregation as he is not allowed to form a row alone if there is space available in the front. The rows need to be straight and compact so that the shoulders of those praying in congregation touch one another.

In order to reach the prayer in time, an individual must make the intention for prayer and perform the *takbîr* before the imam rises from the bowing position of the first unit of prayer, saying "Sami'allâhu liman hamidah." A person who makes the intention of complying with the imam who is still in the bowing position of the first unit of prayer has arrived in time for the first unit of prayer in time. If a latecomer joins the congregation before or in the bowing position of any unit of prayer, then it means he has completed that unit (*rak'ah*) of prayer.

Those who arrive late, and make the intention of complying with the imam in the second, third, or fourth units continue the congregational prayer as usual, but after the imam gives *salâm* at the end of the prayer, the person rises from the sitting position and, proclaiming "Allâhu akbar," completes the missed units of prayer in order, beginning with the first unit.

Therefore, the latecomer who complies with the imam does not give *salâm* together with the imam but stands up to complete the missed units right after the imam gives the *salâm*. While he is in the standing position to perform the units of missed prayers, he must recite *Al-Fâtihah* (and the additional verses of the Qur'ân while performing the first two units of his missed prayer) as he would while praying alone. We should keep in mind that the unit in which the individual complied with the imam is classified as his first unit of prayer, and then the individual must continue the subsequent units accordingly. For example, a person who arrives during the last unit of the night prayer should make the intention of complying with the imam, pronounce the *takbîr*, and continue the prayer without reciting anything else. Then he must remain seated, recite *at-tahiyyât* in the sitting position, and then wait for the imam to give *salâm*. The individual must then stand without giving *salâm* and begin to perform the first unit of prayer that he missed. Reciting *Subhânaka* and *Audhu-Basmala*, then *Al-Fâtihah* and some more verses of the Qur'ân, the individual performs the bowing, prostrations, and recitation of *at-tahiyyât* in the sitting position. Then he stands up to perform the second unit of prayer that he missed. reciting *Al-Fâtihah* and other verses of the Qur'ân. Finally, he stands up to perform the third unit of prayer that he missed and recites only *Al-Fâtihah*, then performs the bowing, prostrations, and recitations of supplications in the final sitting position and gives *salâm* to the right and the left as usual.

Qadâ' Prayer

A prayer executed within the prescribed time is performing the duty of worship, but a prayer performed after the prescribed time is a *qadâ'*, or compensatory prayer.

Performing the prayer within the prescribed time is very important in Islam, thus our religion provides us with the means of convenience. It commands us to pray at all conditions: "Pray in the standing position, and those who are unable to do so can pray in the sitting position, but if you are unable to do so then pray lying down. Those who are in a state of *junub* (major impurity) and cannot find water to perform the rituals of purification can perform the *tayammum* and pray." Even the Muslims who participated in the battles were ordered to take turns in performing prayer. It was also revealed that the first thing Muslims will be accountable for on the Day of Judgment is the prayers.

When is the qadâ' prayer performed?

It is compulsory to perform the *qadâ'* or compensatory prayer for any of the five *fard* prayers that are not performed within the prescribed time. However, compensating for the *witr* prayer is *wâjib* in the Hanafi School. With the exception of the Sunnah units of the morning prayer, any Sunnah prayers that have not been performed within the prescribed times are not compensated for at a later time. In order for the *qadâ'* of the morning prayer to be deemed valid, the Sunnah of the morning prayer must be performed together with the *fard* units of the morning prayer before noon.

Are prayers performed outside the prescribed time accepted?

Those who could not perform the prayer within the prescribed time must execute the missed prayer at the earliest time possible.

Compensating for a missed prayer is also a display of repentance and the means of asking forgiveness. God never rejects those who are truly sincere in their actions. However, neglecting the prayer for no valid excuse is a major sin. Any Muslim who has true affection for the Creator must perform religious duties with devotion and continuity. The Prophet advised us regarding the negligence of prayer: "The first thing people will be accountable for on the Day of Judgment is the prayer. If the prayer is incomplete God will say to His Angels 'Look at My servant's book of deeds. If he performed the supererogatory prayers then complete his obligatory prayers with his supererogatory prayers.'"

When can the qadâ' prayer be performed?

The compensatory prayers can be performed at any time with the exception of the three specific periods in which praying is prohibited. These three times are:

1. The forty five minute period after sunrise.

2. When the sun is at its peak (the 30 minute period before the time prescribed for noon prayer begins).

3. The forty five minute period before the evening prayer begins.

How do we make the intention for performing the qadâ' prayer?

If there is a precise time and day for the *qadâ'* or compensatory prayer, then the prescribed time and day of the prayer must be defined when making the intention for the prayer, for example: "I intend to compensate for the *fard* of last Sunday's noon prayer." However, if there is more than one prayer to compensate for, then the intention should be to the effect of "I intend to compensate for the last morning prayer I was unable to pray for the sake of God."

Supererogatory (Nawafil) Prayers

In addition to the Sunnah of the five prescribed prayers, there were also prayers that the Prophet performed on a regular basis. These prayers are called the *nafl*, or supererogatory, prayers— prayers that are the means of becoming spiritually closer to the Creator. These are some of the optional prayers:

Tahajjud Prayer

Tahajjud is a supererogatory prayer performed after the night prayer and having slept a while. Therefore, it can be performed in the early, middle, or latter part of the night until the morning prayer. This is a prayer that the Prophet performed on a regular basis, a prayer that bears great reward. *Tahajjud* may be executed by performing the minimum two and maximum eight units of prayer. Giving *salâm* at the end of performing every two units of prayer is greater in reward. In one of the hadith the Prophet said: "Observe the *tahajjud* prayer, for it was the practice of the righteous before you; it is the means of coming closer to your Lord, an expiation for your evil deeds, and a shield against sin."

Duha (Forenoon) Prayer

This supererogatory prayer is performed between the period after the sun has fully risen in the morning and until thirty minutes before the time for noon prayer begins. *Duha* prayer is performed by praying at least two or at the most twelve units of prayer. Referring to the *duha* prayer, the Messenger of God said: "Whoever observes the *duha* (forenoon) prayer, with the exception of the rights of others, will be forgiven for all sins even if they are like the foam of the ocean."

Awwâbin Prayer

The *awwâbin* prayer is an optional form of worship. The word *awwâbin* means those who turn to God frequently in prayer.

This is the minimum of two and the maximum six units of prayer, performed after the evening prayer.

Tasbîh Prayer

The prayer of *tasbîh* (glorification) consists of four units, in which *Al-Fâtihah* and some more verses of the Qur'ân are recited in every unit of the prayer. On completion of the recitation of *Al-Fâtihah* and additional verses of the Qur'ân in the first unit, "Subhânallâhi walhamdulillâhi walâ ilâha illallâhu wallâhu akbar" is recited fifteen times while in the standing position. The same *tasbîh* is recited ten times in the bowing position, and then rising from the bowing position is recited another ten times while standing. The individual then prostrates and repeats the *tasbîh* ten times while prostrating, and again in the sitting position, and another ten times in prostration, then rising to the sitting position again recites the *tasbîh* another ten times thus completing the first unit of the prayer. The remaining units are performed in the same manner until the completion of all four units of the prayer.

In addition to the supererogatory prayers stated above, there are also various supererogatory prayers performed on the eclipse of the sun and moon, during times of drought and disaster, after performing ablutions, on entering the mosque, and during the times of difficulty.

Friday (Jumu'ah) Prayer

The Friday (Jumu'ah) prayer is a congregational prayer performed in the mosque at noon on Fridays. Attending the Friday prayers is compulsory for every male Muslim. Those who attend this congregational prayer do not separately perform the normal noon prayer; however, if an individual misses a Friday prayer due to any reason, then he must perform the noon prayer during the time for the noon prayer.

The Friday prayers were prescribed an obligatory act of worship with the revelation of the following verse of the Qur'ân:

> O you who believe! When the call is made for the Prayer on Friday, then move promptly to the remembrance of God (by listening to the sermon and doing the Prayer), and leave off business (and whatever else you may be preoccupied with). This is better for you, if you but knew. (Jumu'ah 62:9)

The Importance of the Friday Prayers

The Friday prayer encourages Muslims to gather and socialize, strengthens the ties of brotherhood, and secures unity and solidarity among the community. Prophet Muhammad, peace and blessings be upon him, greatly emphasized the importance of attending the Friday prayers. The words, "...move promptly to the remembrance of God" in the above verse are words of warning: "Do not underestimate the importance of the Friday prayers, for this prayer is important to Me. Be prompt in attending Friday prayers, and never neglect the prayer due to worldly duties." The Prophet said, "Whoever performs ghusl, attends the Friday prayers, and listens silently and attentively to the imam's sermon will be forgiven for his sins from that Friday until the next, with an addition of three days (ten days in total)."

Who must perform the Friday prayers?

Attending the Friday prayer is compulsory for every Muslim male who is sane, has reached puberty, and is at liberty to do so (those who are politically free).

The Friday prayer is not obligatory for those who are ill or travelling, for children, for women, or for those who are not free. However, those stated above can attend the mosque for the Friday prayer if they wish to do so.

How are the Friday prayers performed?

The Friday prayer is performed at the time prescribed for the daily noon prayer on Fridays. The *Adhân* for the Friday prayer is called from the minaret of the mosque. On entering the mosque, initially the first Sunnah (four units) of the Friday prayer is performed in the same way as the Sunnah of the noon prayer. After the Sunnah prayer, the *adhân* is recited again, only this time inside the mosque, after which the imam begins the sermon. The purpose of the sermon is to explain Islamic subjects to the Muslims; that is, to inform and enlighten the community regarding religion and the world in general. It is necessary to remain quiet and listen to the imam as he gives the sermon. In

one hadith, the Prophet stressed the importance of not speaking during the Friday sermon: "If a person tells somebody next to him to 'Be quiet and listen' while the imam is giving the sermon, he too would have spoken." The sermon is one of the conditions which validates the Friday prayer. The *iqâmah* is recited after the sermon, and two *fard* units of the prayer are performed with the congregation. Prayers of those who arrive in time for the *fard* prayers are also valid. Even if a person reaches the last sitting of the Friday prayer, he rises to the standing position as the imam gives *salâm* at the end of the prayer and performs two units of prayer, thereby validating the Friday prayer.

The two-unit *fard* of the Friday prayer is performed in the same way as the *fard* units of the morning prayer.

As in the case of all the *fard* prayers performed in congregation, when performing the *fard* of the Friday prayer, those complying with the imam do not recite *Al-Fâtihah* or any other verse of the Qur'ân, but while in the standing position following the opening *takbîr*, they only recite *Subhânaka* and *A'ûdhu-Basmala*. They continue to recite the necessary supplications during the bowing, prostrating, and sitting positions as in all the other prayers.

After the *fard* prayer, the four-unit last Sunnah of the Friday prayer is performed in the same way as the first Sunnah of the Friday prayer. Following the last Sunnah of the Friday prayer, there is a prayer consisting of four units called the *Salâtuz-Zuhr*. This is performed in the same way as the *fard* of noon prayer. This is followed by two more units of prayer performed in the same manner as the last Sunnah units of the noon prayer with the intention completing the Sunnah units of the prescribed noon prayer.

Tarâwih Prayer

Tarâwih is a prayer performed during the nights of the month of Ramadan. The Prophet attended to the *tarâwih* prayer without fail, and said: "Whoever spends the night in prayer in Ramadan believing in God and seeking His reward, all his previous sins will be forgiven." It is Sunnah to perform the *tarâwih* prayer even for those who are unable to fast during Ramadan due to illness, journeying, or any other valid reason for which a person is excused from fasting. This prayer can be performed alone or in congregation; however, the reward is much greater for performing the *tarâwih* as a congregational prayer.

How is the tarâwih prayer performed?

The *tarâwih* prayer is performed after the night prayer but before the *witr* prayer. It is not permissible to perform the *tarâwih* before the night prayers are completed.

The *tarâwih* consists of a total of twenty units, and *salâm* may be given at the end of every two or four units. In either case, the units of prayer are continued until all the twenty units are complete.

How to Perform Tarâwih in Congregation

As in the case of praying *tarâwih* alone, if *tarâwih* is to be established as a congregational prayer, it begins after the night prayer.

Initially, the intention for prayer is made: "I intend to comply with the imam to perform the *tarâwih* prayer for the sake of God." Then the prayer begins with the *takbîr*, *Subhânaka* is then recited, and the individual continues the prayer by complying with the imam as in the usual congregational prayers. The imam may give *salâm*s after completing either two or four units.

How to Perform Tarâwih Prayer Alone

The intention for prayer is made, "I intend to perform the *tarâwih* prayers for the sake of God," and then the prayer is performed. If *salâm* is to be pronounced following each two units of prayer, then the prayer is executed in the same way as the Sunnah units of the morning prayer, but if *salâm* is to be given at the end of four units, the prayer is performed in exactly the same way as the first Sunnah of the night prayer. In this case, after the recitation of *at-tahiyyât* in the first sitting of the prayer, the supplications *Allâhumma Salli* and *Allâhumma Bârik* must also be recited.

Prayer of Those Travelling

According to the Islamic faith, a Muslim who leaves home for a journey of ninety kilometers or more and intends to remain at the destination for less than fifteen days is classified as a guest. The traveler shortens a four unit *fard* prayer, praying only two units, whereas the *fard* prayers that consist of two or three units are not shortened but are performed the same as the usual *fard* prayers. Whoever leaves home with the intention of travelling on a journey of ninety kilometers or more performs the shortened prayers upon passing the boundaries of the city or district of residence. On the return journey, travelers must perform the prayers in the normal manner as soon as they enter the boundary of their district or city of habitation, for this is when the journey ends according to Islamic regulations. Prayers are not shortened if a person intends to remain at the destination for more than fifteen days. The Friday prayer is not obligatory for a traveler, but if the individual does attend the Friday prayer, the person will have fulfilled the noon prayer.

'Iyd Prayer

There are two religious festivals called the *'Iyd* of the sacrifice (*'Iydul-Adhâ*) and the *'Iyd* of Ramadan (*'Iydul-Fitr*).

The 'Iyd prayers are performed in congregation, forty five minutes after sunrise on the morning of first day of these religious celebrations. One cannot perform the *'Iyd* prayer alone or make it up at a later time (*qadâ'*). The *'Iyd* prayer is *wâjib* (necessary) and consists of two units of prayer performed without the recitation of the *adhân* or the *iqâmah*. The *'Iyd* prayer is concluded with a sermon given by the imam.

How is the 'Iyd prayer performed?

The intention for prayer is made: "I intend to comply with the imam and perform the prayer of the *'Iydul-Fitr* (or the *'Iydul-Adhâ*) for the sake of God," which is followed by the first *takbîr* pronounced with the imam. *Subhânaka* is recited and then raising the hands, the *takbîr* is pronounced again with the imam, and the hands are lowered to the side of the body. The second *takbîr* is pronounced, and again the hands are lowered to the side of the body. Then the *takbîr* is repeated for the third time in the prayer, but this time the hands are placed on the navel (chest for women) as in the daily prayers. Then the imam recites *Al-Fâtihah* and other verses from the Qur'ân. This is followed by the usual supplications recited during the bowing position and the prostrations, and then the congregation rises to standing position to continue the second unit of prayer. In the second unit, the imam recites *Al-Fâtihah* and verses of the Qur'ân, and the congregation pronounces *takbîr* with the imam and then lowers the hands down beside the body. This is followed by the second and third *takbîr*s, and again the hands are lowered to the side of

the body. Then the forth *takbîr* is pronounced. They bow down and complete the two prostrations as usual. In the last sitting of the prayer, the supplications *at-tahiyyât*, *Allâhumma Salli*, *Allâhumma Bârik* as well as the supplications of *Rabbanâ âtinâ* and *Rabbanâghfirlî* are recited. Then the *salâm* is given to the right and left with the imam, thus concluding the two units of *'Iyd* prayer.

In addition, Muslims must exalt God on the *'Iyd* (festive) days of the sacrifice by pronouncing, *Allâhu akbar*, *Allâhu akbar*; *lâ ilâha illallâhu wallâhu akbar; Allâhu akbar wa lillâhil-hamd* (which means "God is the All-Great, God is the All-Great. There is no deity but God, and God is the All-Great. God is the All-Great and His is all praise"). This *takbîr* of the 'Iyd is pronounced after every prescribed daily prayer after the morning prayer on the day before the 'Iyd of the sacrifice and ends after the afternoon prayer on the fourth day of the 'Iyd.

Funeral Prayer

The funeral (*janâzah*) prayer is a duty performed to ask for the forgiveness of the deceased person's sins. This is an Islamic and also a humanistic duty of all Muslims. If the funeral prayer, which is actually a supplication for deceased Muslims, is attended by some of the community, it eliminates the obligation of performing the prayer for the community on a whole. If nobody attends the funeral prayer, then every Muslim who resides within that district is considered a sinner. Such forms of worship are known as *fard al-kifâyah*, or communal obligation.

How is the funeral prayer performed?

The funeral prayer is performed in the standing position, and with the pronouncing of four *takbîr*s. There are no *rukû*'s (bows) or *sajdah*s (prostrations) during in the funeral prayer. The intention for the prayer is made by specifying the deceased's sex: "I intend to perform the funeral prayer of this deceased (male/female) Muslim and comply with the imam;" then the hands are raised to ear level, the *takbîr* is pronounced with the imam, and the hands are placed on the navel. Then the supplication of *Subhânaka* is recited; "Wa jalla thanâ'uka" should also be included in the supplication of the funeral prayer. Then the second *takbîr* is pronounced with the imam and the supplications *Allâhumma Salli* and *Allâhumma Bârik* are recited; this is followed by the third *takbîr* and the recitation of one of the *janâzah* supplications which were recited by the Prophet (if known). If the individual is not familiar with these supplications of the Prophet, then the *Qunût* supplication, *Rabbanâ âtinâ* or any of the verses bearing supplication from the Qur'ân may be recited. Then the fourth and final *takbîr* is pronounced with the imam, and *salâm* is given to the right and the left, thus concluding the prayer. The hands are not raised after the first *takbîr*. The regulations of the funeral prayer are the same as the other prayers; therefore, whatever invalidates the daily prayers also invalidates the funeral prayer.

The Blessed Days and Nights

As Muslims we are aware that our religious duties and worship are a command from the Creator; therefore, we make every effort possible to obtain His pleasure and strive to earn the eternal bliss of Paradise. Nevertheless, there may be a possibility that our worship is insufficient or that we may have committed a sin either intentionally or unintentionally. The Creator, the Owner of compassion who recognizes His servants' every action, provided us with guidance and various opportunities of eliminating our sins. God the Almighty blessed us with specific days and nights that are much more sacred and greater in reward than others. The Creator bestows His servants a reward of ten, seventy, or even seven hundred times greater accordingly on these sacred days and nights. These days and nights are virtually a precious key which opens the gates leading to the eternal life of bliss, the gates of Paradise, but above all these sacred days and nights are a great opportunity of earning the pleasure of the Creator. These sacred days and nights are:

Mawlid an-Nabî

Prophet Muhammad, peace and blessings be upon him, was born in Mecca on the twentieth of April 571, and the night of the Prophet's birthday is known as *Mawlid an-Nabî*.

The Night of Raghâib

The night of Raghâib is the first Friday night in the month of Rajab. The reasons for this night being known by this particular name is because it is a night in which the Creator's forgiveness and compassion is bountiful, and also because it was one of the nights greatly favored by the Prophet. The abundance of reward for those who spend this night in worship is exceptional. According to reports, the Prophet would perform twelve units of prayer on this holy night.

Mi'râj

On the twenty seventh night of the month of Rajab while the Prophet was in Mecca, he was lead from his home by the Archangel Gabriel and taken on a night journey, the ascension to the Heavens. During this miraculous event known as the Mi'râj, or Ascension, the Prophet travelled to each level of the Heavens, observed Paradise and the Hellfire, and observed the beauty of God without a screen. On this holy night, the five prescribed prayers were deemed obligatory upon Muslims. This is why the Prophet said: "Prayer is the ascension of a believer." Prayer is the time when the servant stands in the presence of his Lord. Therefore every Muslim must make an effort to spend this night praying, glorifying God, reciting the blessings and peace of the Creator upon His devoted servant and Messenger, reciting the Qur'ân, and sincerely repenting for any past sins.

The Night of Bara'ah

The Night of Bara'ah is on the fifteenth night of the month of Sha'ban. Bara'ah means salvation, and this night is an opportunity to purify oneself from sin and reach salvation. This is the night in which the good deeds and the bad deeds performed throughout the entire year are recorded, and the destiny of every individual is determined. Spending this night in worship and repentance is the means of successfully completing the record for the entire year's deeds. Indicating the importance of spending this night in worship, the Prophet said:

> Let all of you spend the night of mid-Sha'ban (Bara'ah) in worship and its day fasting. For God descends to the nearest heaven of the world (i.e. God honors the skies of the world with His Mercy) during this night from sunset, and asks: "Is there no one asking forgiveness that I may forgive them? Is there no one asking sustenance that I may grant them sustenance? Is there no one under trial that I may relieve them? Is there not such-and-such, and so on" until dawn rises.

The Night of Qadr

The Night of Qadr (Power) is the night in which the single most important event in history unfolded as Archangel Gabriel descended with the Holy Qur'ân to reveal it to God's Messenger. Thus this night is the most sacred night. Indeed, God Almighty distinguishes this most blessed night of the year as being *"better than a thousand months"* (Qadr 97:3) and describes it as being imbued with *"peace until the rise of the morn"* (Qadr 97:5). On the Night of Qadr, so many Angels descend from the Heavens that the Divine light spreads throughout the entire earth.

The Prophet said, "The person who sincerely believes in the blessings of the Night of Qadr and prays during the night will be forgiven their past sins." He stated that the Night of Qadr is to be found in the last ten days of Ramadan. Therefore, the sincere believers should stay up in prayer and worship during the last ten days of Ramadan, on which the Night of Qadr could fall. On such holy days and nights of abundance, we should all benefit from this great opportunity by spending our time in worship, reciting the Qur'ân, repenting for our sins, supplicating to God, and seeking forgiveness. In addition to this, we should attend the meetings and sermons relating to God, Islam, and the Prophet whenever possible.

HALF OF PATIENCE

Fasting

"The one who fasts has two occasions of joy, one at the time of breaking their fast, and the other at the time when they will meet their Lord; then they will be pleased because of their fasting." Hadith

What is fasting? What is the purpose of fasting?

Fasting, or *sawm* in Arabic, is abstaining from the cravings of the carnal soul during the period beginning before the break of dawn and until sunset with the aim of disciplining the desires by consciously refraining from eating, drinking, and sexual relations. Fasting during the month of Ramadan, which is the ninth month of the Islamic lunar calendar, is one of the five pillars of Islam deemed obligatory upon the Muslims in this verse of Qur'ân: *"O you who believe! Prescribed for you is the Fast, as it was prescribed for those before you, so that you may deserve God's protection (against the temptations of your carnal soul) and attain piety"* (Baqarah 2:183).

God Almighty has made the reward for fasting greater than the reward for any other form of worship. The following Hadith Qudsi highlights the true value of fasting in the eyes of God and the greatness of the reward that awaits those who fast: "Every good deed will be rewarded from ten to seven hundred times, except fasting. Fasting is for Me, and I shall reward it (without measure)."

Performing any form of worship consciously is obviously crucial for the soundness of belief, but is also very important for us to maintain our faith. As in the case of all forms of worship, there are various reasons for the fast of Ramadan being prescribed compulsory upon the Muslims. The purpose of fasting is not to make people endure hunger; the aim of fasting is restraining from evil actions, maintaining spiritual discipline, and con-

trolling the soul's desires for God's sake. Fasting is the means of disciplining our bodies, our souls, and our emotions and, therefore, encourages Muslims to become virtuous, mature, charitable, kind, and compassionate humans.

What are the advantages of fasting?

Committing a sin or mistake is a constant source of concern for any devoted believer. In this sense, fasting is a great blessing for a Muslim, a form of spiritual purification which relieves apprehension and fills the heart with tranquility. The Prophet said, "Whoever fasts during Ramadan with faith and seeking his reward from God will have his past sins forgiven." Fasting is a shield that prevents us from sinning and protects us against evil actions. On one hand, the joy of forgiveness for past sins, and on the other, the fear of the alleviation of rewards due to sin obviously makes those who fast even more apprehensive and more sensitive to avoiding sin. In other words, fasting enhances the character of a Muslim. Fasting is the means of salvation and forgiveness, a spiritual reminder that we are in the presence of God at all times. Those who fast are embraced in a constant emotion of worship, the spiritual bond drawing us closer to the Creator and protecting us in everything we do. As the Prophet said, "Fasting is a shield." And the constant feeling of worship arouses our awareness of being in the presence of the Creator. All of us appreciate the blessings bestowed by God,

but we tend to display our duty of gratitude for these blessings greater at the time of hunger and thirst. By abstaining from the blessings God prescribed lawful during the period which He forbids, we are reminded that our duty is to abide by God's commands; therefore, we become more aware of our servitude and our duties as Muslims. Fasting teaches us patience, for we abstain from eating and drinking not by force, but by our own willpower. As the Prophet said, "Fasting is one half of patience, and patience is one half of faith."

How should a fasting Muslim act?

Fasting is not only abstaining from eating and drinking, or abandoning specific worldly pleasures, it also entails avoiding any kind of sin and bad behavior. Just as a fasting person refrains from the pleasures of eating and drinking, he must also protect the tongue from lying, slander, and gossip; the hands from unlawful or evil actions; the ears from heeding to anything sinful; the feet from straying towards sin; and the heart and mind from evil thoughts and intentions. Of course, a fasting person who refrains from the lawful pleasures of his own home with total sincerity, and awareness of the fast, will most certainly abstain from sin or that which is prescribed unlawful. As the Prophet said, "The best of the believers is the one who, when you look at him, you remember God."

Who is obliged to fast during the month of Ramadan?

Fasting during the month of Ramadan is compulsory for every male and female who:

1 – Are Muslims

2 – Are sane and conscious of their actions

3 – Have reached puberty

What are the conditions of the fast's validity?

1 – The intention of fasting.

2 - Women not being in the state of menstruation or post-natal bleeding.

What are the times of fasting?

The fast begins just before dawn (*imsâk*) and continues until sunset. The beginning of the fast, called *imsâk*, is the time when the morning prayer begins. *Imsâk* marks the end of the time for having the predawn meal (*sahûr*) just before the first light of dawn. *Iftâr* is when the fast ends at sunset, when the time for the evening prayer begins. Those who abstain from food and drink the whole day break the fast at sunset, and they may continue to eat and drink until the beginning of the morning prayer. The meal eaten in the evening to break the fast is called *iftâr* and those who complete the fast feel a sense of pleasure and contentment of fulfilling their duty to God. But the greatest pleasure of all is when Muslims go before the Lord on the Day of Judgment to receive their rewards for fasting. The Prophet said, "The one who fasts has two occasions of joy, one at the time of breaking their fast, and the other at the time when they will meet their Lord; then they will be pleased because of their fasting."

Those who intend to fast eat a meal before the first light of dawn known as the *sahûr* meal. The Prophet told us, "Get up (and eat) at *sahûr*, for there is blessing in *sahûr*." Indeed, the *sahûr* time is blessed and fruitful in many ways: The person who has the *sahûr* meal observes the tradition of the Prophet and attains enough energy and strength for the fast and other forms of worship throughout the day ahead. *Sahûr* is the best time to supplicate, to perform prayers, to glorify God, and to recite the Qur'ân because good deeds observed at that hour of the night have been reported to be more welcome than the rest of the day. Indeed, it is a time when all supplications made to God are accepted.

Though it is more virtuous to make the intention for the fast at night following the pre-dawn meal, the intention can be made at any time from sunset right after having the *iftâr* dinner until forty five minutes before noon prayer the following day. However, the intention for the fast can only be made after dawn if the individual has not eaten or drunk anything nor done anything that invalidates fasting since the time of *imsâk*, or the break of the dawn. As every day of Ramadan is classified as an independent worship, the intention for fasting must be renewed daily.

Under what conditions can the fast be delayed?

A person is permitted to delay the fast until a later date due to any of the conditions listed below:

1. A serious illness.

2. Travelling on a journey of ninety kilometers or more.

3. When fasting may cause a threat to a person's life.

4. If a woman is pregnant or breastfeeding.

5. If hunger or thirst is so the extreme that it may cause damage to the health.

6. The elderly who are too weak or sick to endure the fast.

What should those unable to fast during Ramadan do?

A person unable to fast during the month of Ramadan due to any of the reasons stated above must compensate for every day of the fast missed when the hindrance no longer applies. Those who are exempt from fasting due to incurable health problems or those too old and frail to fast must compensate for every day of the fast missed by providing a needy person with either food or money sufficient to satisfy a human from morning until night. However, if this person recovers at a later time, these fasts must be compensated for by fasting one day for each of the missed fasts.

Is abandoning the fast punishable?

Abandoning the fast with no valid excuse is a great sin. Every day of the fast that was abandoned after fasting has begun must be compensated (*qadâ'*), and expiation (*kaffârah*) for the fast is also necessary for those who deliberately eat and drink while observing the fast of Ramadan.

What are qadâ' and kaffârah?

Certain conditions that invalidate the fast only require compensation of the fast, whereas other conditions require both *qadâ'* and *kaffârah* (expiation). Compensation for the fasts which were not held or were forced to abandon for a valid reason must be performed day for day after the month of Ramadan. Kaffârah is a fast of expiation for intentionally or voluntarily breaking the fast with no valid excuse, a penalty of fasting that must be executed with no intervals for two consecutive months, and one day must also be held in compensation for the abandoned fast.

What are the conditions that invalidate the fast and require both qadâ' and kaffârah?

Doing one of the following with no valid excuse or under no compulsion or intentionally requires both a sixty-day *kaffârah* and a make-up day (*qadâ'*):

1. Eating, drinking or swallowing any kind of medicine.

2. Sexual relations or masturbation.

3. Intentionally swallowing rain, snow or hail that entered the mouth by accident.

4. Smoking cigarettes, cigars, water pipes, or inhaling the intoxicating smoke of any other herb.

5. Taking anything, even as small as a sesame seed into the mouth and then swallow it, including swallowing a small amount of salt.

A person who does any of the things mentioned above with no valid excuse, must fast for two consecutive months as a punishment for intentionally breaking the fast, and also compensate by fasting for the missed day.

What are the conditions that invalidate the fast but only require a make-up day (qadâ')?

1. Eating things that are not normally eaten by or that do not appeal to human beings, such as eating things like paper, stone, soil, iron, gold, and silver, swallowing an empty walnut or eating an olive pip that is not usually eaten (eating pips that are usually eaten requires *kaffârah*), or eating a large amount of salt at one time.

2. Swallowing saliva that has changed color due to the dye from cotton placed in the mouth.

3. Unintentionally swallowing rain or snow which entered the mouth by accident.

4. Breaking the fast under severe physical torture or force.

5. Swallowing the remains of food no larger than a chickpea that was stuck between the teeth.

6. If water is swallowed accidently when taking water into the mouth and nostrils while performing ablutions.

7. Eating or drinking after assuming that the fast is invalid after forgetfully eating and drinking.

8. Vomiting intentionally; even if the vomit is less than a mouthful, the fast is invalid.

9. Swallowing a mouthful of vomit, or that which was intentionally vomited.

10. Intentionally breathing in smoke, but the fast is not invalid if breathed in unintentionally. (*Kaffârah*, or expiation of the fast, is necessary if the smoke breathed in intentionally is the smoke from a cigarette, cigar, or water pipe).

11. Eating or drinking under the assumption that the sun had set before it actually did.

12. Eating or drinking in the early morning wrongly assuming that there was still time until the fast began.

13. Breaking a fast other than the fasts of Ramadan. Only compensating for the particular day is necessary if a fast, other than the fasts of Ramadan, is abandoned.

14. If a person eats and drinks but did not make the intention of fasting on a day during Ramadan. If the intention for the fast is made, and the individual eats and drinks intentionally, then expiation (*kaffârah*) for the fast is necessary. However, if an individual eats and drinks but did not make the intention of fasting, only compensating for that particular fast is necessary.

15. Using medicine, suppositories, or an injection administered for health reasons.

16. If medication or any substance applied to a wound enters the body.

17. Inhaling medication through the nostrils.

18. If any water that is taken in the mouth or the nostrils enters the throat or nasal passage by accident.

What does not invalidate the fast?

1. If a person forgets he is fasting and eats or drinks. The Prophet said, "If a person eats or drinks due to forgetfulness, he should continue the fast for it was God who fed him and gave him the drink." A person who eats or drinks due to forgetfulness should empty the food or drink from the mouth, rinse the mouth with water as soon as he remembers that he is fasting, and then continue the fast as usual.

2. If smoke dust, or flies enters the mouth accidently.

3. If a person vomits unintentionally.

4. Becoming spiritually impure while sleeping (due to wet dreams) or due to the thought or sight of something.

5. If a person becomes spiritually impure at night, but does not perform the *ghusl* until after dawn.

6. If the head is submerged in water, and water enters the ears. Therefore, the water that leaks into the ears when bathing does not invalidate the fast.

7. Swallowing a piece of food smaller than a chickpea which remained between the teeth from the pre-dawn (*sahûr*) meal.

8. Swallowing one's own saliva or inhaling mucus; however, swallowing saliva removed from the mouth invalidates the fast.

9. Swallowing phlegm.

10. Putting eye drops in the eyes.

11. Giving blood.

12. Applying kohl to the eyes.

13. Applying medicine, cream or ointment to the outer body (even if substances are absorbed into the body by the pores of the skin, provided that the substance applied to a wound does not enter the body). Similarly, water that is used for cleaning and washing up does not invalidate the fast either, for these are all absorbed through pores of the skin, not the mouth or nose.

THE BRIDGE OF THE RELIGION

Charity

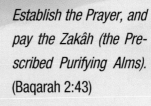

Establish the Prayer, and pay the Zakâh (the Prescribed Purifying Alms).
(Baqarah 2:43)

What Is Zakâh?

Zakâh is a form of charity, a certain amount of the wealth distributed every year by the wealthy Muslims to the poor for the sake of God. *Zakâh* is also one of the pillars of Islam like the daily prayers. While, in the words of God's Messenger, the prayer is Islam's main pillar, the *Zakâh* is its bridge, for the *Zakâh* not only brings the social strata closer to each other and fills in the gaps already formed between them and their members, but also stops such gaps from forming.

Giving charity was made obligatory upon the Muslims in the second year of the holy migration before the fast of Ramadan was deemed compulsory. Unlike the prayers and fasting, which are physical forms of worship, charity is a form of worship executed with wealth. God the Almighty ordained *Zakâh* obligatory upon the Muslims with the revelation of this verse of the Qur'ân: *"Establish the Prayer, and pay the Prescribed Purifying Alms (the Zakâh)"* (Baqarah 2:43).

Just as the five daily prayers are the pillar of a believer's religious life, the prescribed charity of *Zakâh* is the pillar of the social lives of Muslims. There would be no establishment of order and unity among individuals in societies where the Islamic command of charity is not practiced. The collaboration and solidarity between the wealthy and the poor would diminish, and the sense of affection and respect for others would totally disappear.

Who must give Zakâh?

The conditions which deem a person responsible for giving this prescribed purifying charity are:

1. The person giving charity must be a Muslim, must be free (not a slave), sane, and have reached puberty.

2. The person giving charity must own more wealth than personal debts and basic needs. Giving charity is not compulsory upon those who do not own the stated amount of wealth.

The specific amount of wealth prescribed in Islam for charity deemed compulsory upon a person varies according to the type of wealth or commodity. Another condition of distributing charity is that the person must own the goods or wealth for an entire year. One of the conditions that validates *Zakâh* is that the individual must have the intention of giving charity in the heart.

What commodities do we pay Zakâh for, and how much do we pay?

1. One fortieth of any cash or the like equivalent to the value of eighty grams of gold.

2. One fortieth of any silver which is five hundred and sixty grams or more.

3. One fortieth of the value of any trade merchandise which is equivalent to the value of eighty grams of gold or more.

4. One goat or sheep for every forty goats or sheep.

5. One cow for every thirty cattle.

6. One sheep must be given in charity for every five camels.

To whom should the Zakâh be distributed?

The reply to this question is clearly defined in this verse of the Qur'ân:

> *The Prescribed Purifying Alms (Zakâh) are meant only for the poor, and the destitute, and those in charge of collecting (and administering) them, and those whose hearts are to be won over, and to free those in bondage, and to help those over-burdened with debt, and in God's cause, and for the wayfarer (in need of help). This is an ordinance from God. God is All-Knowing, All-Wise.* (Tawbah 9:60)

Sadaqah

What is sadaqah?

Encompassing a greater area than that of the obligatory alms of *Zakâh*, *sadaqah* can be money, goods, education, or anything given for the sake of God to the poor as a form of voluntary charity. There are many benefits of giving *sadaqah* both in this world and the hereafter. *Sadaqah* is the expiation of sin, a shield against the flames of the Hellfire, and it also wards off affliction and disaster. In the following hadith, God's Messenger has drawn attention to

the broad extent of *sadaqah* and underlined its importance, even if it be a tiny portion, in making amends for a person's wrongs, along with providing a shield against the torment of punishment: "Protect yourselves from hellfire, even if it be with half a date."

If Muslims are asked for help of any kind, they should never reject the request and should always try to help to the best of their ability. Any *sadaqah* given in secret bears greater reward, as the Prophet said in one of the hadith: "Three things are accounted among the treasures of righteousness, and one of them is giving charity in secret."

What is sadaqatul-fitr?

Sadaqatul-fitr is charity given to the poor at the end of Ramadan, a charity obligatory upon every Muslim in possession of a certain amount of wealth exceeding the basic needs. *Fitr* is the charity that is given by a Muslim as a sign of gratitude and praise, and with the aspiration of obtaining reward.

Fitr is distributed during Ramadan and must be given before the 'Iyd prayer on the first day of the 'Iyd celebrations. The *fitr* should reach the poor and needy before the 'Iyd prayer so they can acquire the needs of their families and so they too can experience joy and happiness on this day of celebrations. The *fitr* should first be distributed to people in need among the family or community of the one giving the *fitr*.

Every year in the month of Ramadan, *fitr* is distributed according to the amounts defined in Islam or by the heads of local religious institutions. As with any form of charity or worship, the individual's intention to give fitr is necessary; however, it is not necessary to say to the poor that you give the goods or money as *sadaqah* when distributing it. Although it is not permitted to distribute one person's *fitr* among several poor people, the *fitr* of several people may be given to one needy person. The head of the family is responsible for giving fitr for his spouse and children.

HOLY JOURNEY TO
THE HOUSE OF GOD

Hajj

*"Pilgrimage to the House
is a duty owed to God by
all who can afford a way
to it."* (Âl 'Imrân 3:97)

What is Hajj?

H*ajj* is the pilgrimage to Mecca, the journey made to the Ka'bah and visits to certain holy places to perform the pre-scribed acts of worship by Muslims at a particular time of the year. *Hajj*, or the pilgrimage to Mecca, is one of the five pillars of Islam. *Hajj* was made obligatory upon the Muslims during the ninth year of the holy migration. The obligation of *Hajj* is defined in this verse of the Qur'ân: *"...Pilgrimage to the House is a duty owed to God by all who can afford a way to it..."* (Âl 'Imrân 3:97)

The rewards of performing *Hajj* once in a lifetime, for those who have the financial means and physical capability, are numerous, and these words of the Prophet are more than significant in con-veying the abundance of the holy pilgrimage: "Whoever performs the *Hajj* and does not commit obscenity or transgression, he returns purified from sin just like the day his mother gave birth to him."

Hajj Awakens Humans to the Joy of Servitude

By nature, every human feels the need of demonstrating their worship, their servitude to the Creator. *Hajj* is a form of worship that truly gives believers the opportunity to expose humbleness, to express devotedness as servants, and to demonstrate gratitude before the Creator for all the blessings He bestowed. Those who perform the *Hajj* leave all worldly bonds behind; they abandon wealth, possessions, position and status, and turn to the Creator in humbleness. Standing in total submission before the One of eternal power and might, the believer expresses absolute devotion and worship to God, which in turn awakens the believer to the joy and pleasures of servitude.

Hajj Is Clear Evidence That Every Human Is Equal in the Eyes of the Creator

Hajj is a form of worship that brings millions of Muslims together every year regardless of race, language, color, nation, culture, position, or status. Portraying an inspiring scene of brotherhood and equality, the millions of Muslims from all walks of life gather together for the same purpose, in worship and submission to the Creator. Dressed identically, the wealthy Muslims alongside the poor, the powerful integrated with the weak, all enduring the same difficulties, but even more important, all experiencing the discipline of equality and brotherhood. *Hajj* is total submission, a form of worship that makes the rich stand together, shoulder to shoulder on mount Arafat supplicating together, or circling the Ka'bah side by side with the deprived that can barely provide for their families. *Hajj* teaches Muslims not to boast regarding their position, status, wealth or possessions. It teaches them to gather and integrate according to the Islamic boundaries of brotherhood and to never forget the Day of Reckoning.

Hajj Increases Devotedness to Islam

The journey to this sacred place, the land where the Islamic faith emerged and later spread following the years of hardship and suffering by the Prophet Muhammad, peace and blessings be upon him, and his devoted Companions, this sacred place where the first verses of the Qur'ân were revealed, a holy land that has been a place visited by many Prophets since the Prophet Adam, strengthens the spiritual emotions of a Muslim and increases their devotion to Islam.

Hajj Is Patience and Gratification

By performing the worship of *Hajj*, a Muslim displays gratification to the Lord for health and accomplishments and for the wealth and possessions bestowed by God. The Muslims who perform *Hajj* must display patience and tolerance, endure hardships, and confront difficulties. They develop the abilities of acting together as a group, performing the same actions together in huge crowds, integration, and helping others while adapting to the specific rules and regulations.

Who should attend Hajj?

Hajj is compulsory for those who conform with the conditions below:

1. The sane and conscious.

2. They must be Muslim.

3. They must have reached puberty.

4. Those who are free (not enslaved).

5. Those who know that *Hajj* is obligatory.

6. They must have the means to perform the journey and provide for both themselves, for their families and whoever else they may be responsible for until their return from *Hajj*.

7. They must reach *Hajj* in due time for the rituals of worship.

8. The journey for *Hajj* must be safe.

9. They must be healthy humans.

What is 'Umrah?

'Umrah* is visiting the Ka'bah, Mecca, Medina, and the other sacred places visited during the holy pilgrimage outside the *Hajj* season. In fact, the *'Umrah* worship is performed in the close vicinity of the Ka'bah. It is composed of entering into *ihrâm*, or the state of consecration for the pilgrimage worship, at any time of the year, except the *Hajj* season, and coming out of the state of *ihrâm* after performing the *tawâf* (circumambulation) of the Ka'bah, the *sa'y* (striding between the hillocks of Safa and Marwa), and shaving (or shortening) the hair. Performing *'Umrah* is a sunnah act of worship.

Sacrifice: The Mount for Crossing the Sirat Bridge

The Meaning of the Sacrifice

The sacrifice is offered at a particular time of the year (on the first, second, or third day of the *'Iydul-Adhâ*, the festival of sacrifice) with the intention of worship and obtaining reward from the Creator. Sacrificing an animal is a *wâjib* (necessary) form of worship which is executed with an individual's wealth. The sacrifice is a display of

our devotion, a demonstration of our gratitude for all the blessings God generously bestows upon us. The Prophet said: "The one who has the means but does not perform the sacrifice may not approach our mosque," expressing just how important the duty of sacrificing an animal is for those who have the means to do so.

Who should sacrifice an animal?

Sacrificing an animal is obligatory for those who conform with the conditions stated below:

1. The person must be a Muslim.
2. Must have reached puberty.
3. Must be sane.
4. Must be free (not enslaved).
5. Is not travelling or a guest.
6. Must have sufficient wealth to sacrifice an animal.

When is the animal sacrificed?

The animal is usually sacrificed on the first, second, or third day of the 'Iydul-Adhâ, the festival of sacrifice. This worship of offering a sacrifice for the sake of God can be fulfilled any time during the 'Iyd of the sacrifice until the evening prayer on the third day of the 'Iyd; however, it is more advisable to sacrifice the animal on the first day of the 'Iyd.

Which animals can be sacrificed?

Only sheep, goats, cattle, buffalo, and camels can be sacrificed. The sheep and goats must have reached one year, cattle and buffalo two, and camels five years. If a six month old sheep is larger than average and looks more like an animal of a year old, it may be sacrifice, whereas goats must reach a year old before being sacrificed. A sheep or goat can only be sacrificed by one person, whereas up to seven people can sacrifice a cow, buffalo, or camel jointly. Animals that have damaged or no horns and that are slightly lame or have teeth missing can be sacrificed.

A Prayer of Hope

Every form of worship ordained by God as a duty upon all Muslims is embodied by the practices of the Prophet, who represents an ideal for all humanity to aspire to. In the Qur'ân, God Almighty addresses the Prophet with the words: *"You are surely of a sublime character, and do act by a sublime pattern of conduct"* (Qalam 68:4), guiding us to acknowledge His Messenger, Prophet Muhammad, as the most excellent example to follow in every aspect of our lives.

If we sincerely seek God's good pleasure and become His servants *"whom He loves, and who love Him"* (Mâedah 5:54), we should follow the perfect example of His Messenger in both

worship and sublime character. Love of God requires loving His most beloved servant and Messenger. As the following verse points out, loving the Prophet shows itself by following him and designing our lives according to the practice, or Sunnah, of the Prophet in all respects: *"Say (to them, O Messenger): 'If you indeed love God, then follow me, so that God will love you and forgive you your sins'"* (Âl 'Imrân 3:31). Living a life of worship and performing every act of worship in accordance with the example of the Prophet will lead us to taking him as a role model in every aspect of our lives and thus to adopting his sublime conduct and character.

Inshâllah, we will be among those members of the community of the Prophet who follow his sublime example in our daily lives and become people whom God loves, and who love Him.

APPENDIX

SHORT SŪRAHS AND THE PRAYERS

SŪRAH AL-FĀTIHAH

بِسْمِ اللهِ الرَّحْمٰنِ الرَّحِيمِ

اَلْحَمْدُ للهِ رَبِّ الْعَالَمِينَ ۞ اَلرَّحْمٰنِ الرَّحِيمِ ۞

مَالِكِ يَوْمِ الدِّينِ ۞ إِيَّاكَ نَعْبُدُ وَإِيَّاكَ نَسْتَعِينُ ۞

اِهْدِنَا الصِّرَاطَ الْمُسْتَقِيمَ ۞ صِرَاطَ الَّذِينَ أَنْعَمْتَ عَلَيْهِمْ

غَيْرِ الْمَغْضُوبِ عَلَيْهِمْ وَلاَ الضَّالِّينَ ۞

In the Name of Allah, the All-Merciful, the All-Compassionate

1. In the Name of Allah, the All-Merciful, the All-Compassionate. 2. All praise and gratitude (whoever gives them to whomever for whatever reason and in whatever way from the first day of creation until eternity) are for Allah, the Lord of the worlds, 3. The All-Merciful, the All-Compassionate, 4. The Master of the Day of Judgment. 5. You alone do We worship, and from You alone do we seek help. 6. Guide us to the Straight Path, 7. The Path of those whom You have favored, not of those who have incurred (Your) wrath (punishment and condemnation), nor of those who are astray.

SŪRAH AL-FĪL

بِسْمِ اللهِ الرَّحْمَنِ الرَّحِيمِ

أَلَمْ تَرَ كَيْفَ فَعَلَ رَبُّكَ بِأَصْحَابِ الْفِيلِ ۝ أَلَمْ يَجْعَلْ كَيْدَهُمْ فِي تَضْلِيلٍ ۝ وَأَرْسَلَ عَلَيْهِمْ طَيْرًا أَبَابِيلَ ۝ تَرْمِيهِمْ بِحِجَارَةٍ مِنْ سِجِّيلٍ ۝ فَجَعَلَهُمْ كَعَصْفٍ مَأْكُولٍ ۝

In the Name of Allah, the All-Merciful, the All-Compassionate

1. Have you considered how your Lord dealt with the people of the Elephant? 2. Did He not bring their evil scheme to nothing? 3. He sent down upon them flocks of birds (unknown in the land), 4. Shooting them with bullet-like stones of baked clay (an emblem of the punishment due to them); 5. And so He rendered them like a field of grain devoured and trampled.

SŪRAH QURAYSH

بِسْمِ اللهِ الرَّحْمٰنِ الرَّحِيمِ

لِإِيلَافِ قُرَيْشٍ ۝ إِيلَافِهِمْ رِحْلَةَ الشِّتَآءِ وَالصَّيْفِ ۝
فَلْيَعْبُدُوا رَبَّ هٰذَا الْبَيْتِ ۝ اَلَّذِىٓ اَطْعَمَهُمْ مِنْ جُوعٍ
وَاٰمَنَهُمْ مِنْ خَوْفٍ ۝

In the Name of Allah, the All-Merciful, the All-Compassionate

1. (At least) for (Allah's constant) favor of concord and security to the Quraysh, 2. Their concord and security in their winter and summer journeys, 3. Let them worship the Lord of this House (the Ka'bah), 4. Who has provided them with food against hunger, and made them safe from fear.

SŪRAH AL-MĀ'ŪN

بِسْمِ اللهِ الرَّحْمٰنِ الرَّحِيمِ

أَرَأَيْتَ الَّذِى يُكَذِّبُ بِالدِّينِ ۞ فَذٰلِكَ الَّذِى يَدُعُّ الْيَتِيمَ ۞
وَلاَ يَحُضُّ عَلٰى طَعَامِ الْمِسْكِينِ ۞ فَوَيْلٌ لِلْمُصَلِّينَ ۞
اَلَّذِينَ هُمْ عَنْ صَلاَتِهِمْ سَاهُونَ ۞ اَلَّذِينَ هُمْ يُرَآؤُنَ ۞
وَيَمْنَعُونَ الْمَاعُونَ ۞

In the Name of Allah, the All-Merciful, the All-Compassionate

1. Have you ever considered one who denies the Last Judgment? 2. That is he who repels the orphan, 3. And does not urge the feeding of the destitute. 4. And woe to those worshippers (denying the Judgment), 5. Those who are unmindful in their Prayers, 6. Those who want to be seen and noted (for their acts of worship), 7. Yet deny all assistance (to their fellowmen).

SŪRAH AL-KAWTHAR

إِنَّا اَعْطَيْنَاكَ الْكَوْثَرَ ۞ فَصَلِّ لِرَبِّكَ وَانْحَرْ ۞
إِنَّ شَانِئَكَ هُوَ الْأَبْتَرُ ۞

In the Name of Allah, the All-Merciful, the All-Compassionate

1. We have surely granted you (unceasing) abundant good;
2. So pray to your Lord, and sacrifice (for Him in thank-
fulness). 3. Surely it is the one who offends you who is cut
off (from unceasing good, including posterity).

SŪRAH AL-KĀFIRŪN

بِسْمِ اللَّهِ الرَّحْمَٰنِ الرَّحِيمِ

قُلْ يَا أَيُّهَا الْكَافِرُونَ ۝ لَا أَعْبُدُ مَا تَعْبُدُونَ ۝
وَلَا أَنتُمْ عَابِدُونَ مَا أَعْبُدُ ۝ وَلَا أَنَا عَابِدٌ مَّا عَبَدتُّمْ ۝
وَلَا أَنتُمْ عَابِدُونَ مَا أَعْبُدُ ۝ لَكُمْ دِينُكُمْ وَلِيَ دِينِ ۝

In the Name of Allah, the All-Merciful, the All-Compassionate

1. Say: "O you unbelievers (who obstinately reject faith)!
2. "I do not, nor ever will, worship that which you worship. 3. "Nor are you those who ever worship what I worship. 4. "Nor am I one who do and will ever worship that which you have ever worshipped. 5. "And nor are you those who do and will ever worship what I ever worship. 6. "You have your religion (with whatever it will bring you), and I have my religion (with whatever it will bring me).

SŪRAH AN-NASR

إِذَا جَاءَ نَصْرُ اللهِ وَالْفَتْحُ ۝

وَرَأَيْتَ النَّاسَ يَدْخُلُونَ فِي دِينِ اللهِ أَفْوَاجًا ۝

فَسَبِّحْ بِحَمْدِ رَبِّكَ وَاسْتَغْفِرْهُ إِنَّهُ كَانَ تَوَّابًا ۝

In the Name of Allah, the All-Merciful, the All-Compassionate

1. *When Allah's help comes, and victory (which is a door to further victories),* **2.** *And you see people entering Allah's Religion in throngs,* **3.** *Then glorify your Lord with His praise, and ask Him for forgiveness, for He surely is One Who returns repentance with liberal forgiveness and additional reward.*

SŪRAH TABBAT

بِسْمِ اللهِ الرَّحْمٰنِ الرَّحِيمِ

تَبَّتْ يَدَآ أَبِى لَهَبٍ وَتَبَّ ۝ مَآ أَغْنٰى عَنْهُ مَالُهُ وَمَا كَسَبَ ۝ سَيَصْلٰى نَارًا ذَاتَ لَهَبٍ ۝ وَامْرَأَتُهُ حَمَّالَةَ الْحَطَبِ ۝ فِى جِيدِهَا حَبْلٌ مِنْ مَسَدٍ ۝

In the Name of Allah, the All-Merciful, the All-Compassionate

1. May both hands of Abū Lahab be ruined, and is ruined himself! 2. His wealth has not availed him, nor his gains. 3. He will enter a flaming Fire to roast; 4. And (with him) his wife, carrier of firewood (and of evil tales and slander), 5. Around her neck will be a halter of strongly twisted rope.

SŪRAH AL-IKHLĀS

قُلْ هُوَ اللّٰهُ أَحَدٌ ۞ اَللّٰهُ الصَّمَدُ ۞
لَمْ يَلِدْ وَلَمْ يُولَدْ ۞ وَلَمْ يَكُنْ لَهُ كُفُوًا أَحَدٌ ۞

In the Name of Allah, the All-Merciful, the All-Compassionate

*1. Say: "He – (He is) Allah, (Who is) the Unique One of
Absolute Oneness. 2. "Allah – (Allah is He Who is) the
Eternally-Besought-of-All (Himself being in need of nothing). 3. "He begets not, nor is He begotten. 4. "And com-
parable to Him there is none."*

SŪRAH AL-FALAQ

بِسْمِ اللهِ الرَّحْمَنِ الرَّحِيمِ

قُلْ أَعُوذُ بِرَبِّ الْفَلَقِ ۝ مِنْ شَرِّ مَا خَلَقَ ۝

وَمِنْ شَرِّ غَاسِقٍ إِذَا وَقَبَ ۝ وَمِنْ شَرِّ النَّفَّاثَاتِ فِى الْعُقَدِ ۝

وَمِنْ شَرِّ حَاسِدٍ إِذَا حَسَدَ ۝

In the Name of Allah, the All-Merciful, the All-Compassionate

1. Say: "I seek refuge in the Lord of the daybreak, 2. "From the evil of what He has created; 3. "And from the evil of the darkness (of night) when it overspreads; 4. "And from the evil of the witches who blow on knots (to cast a spell); 5. "And from the evil of the envious one when he envies."

SŪRAH AN-NĀS

بِسْمِ اللهِ الرَّحْمنِ الرَّحِيمِ

قُلْ أَعُوذُ بِرَبِّ النَّاسِ ۞ مَلِكِ النَّاسِ ۞
إِلهِ النَّاسِ ۞ مِنْ شَرِّ الْوَسْوَاسِ الْخَنَّاسِ ۞
الَّذِي يُوَسْوِسُ فِي صُدُورِ النَّاسِ ۞ مِنَ الْجِنَّةِ وَالنَّاسِ ۞

In the Name of Allah, the All-Merciful, the All-Compassionate

1. Say: "I seek refuge in the Lord of humankind, 2. "The Sovereign of humankind, 3. "The Deity of humankind, 4. "From the evil of the sneaking whisperer (the satan), 5. "Who whispers into the hearts of humankind, 6. "Of jinn and humankind."

ÂYAT AL-KURSÎ

بِسْمِ اللهِ الرَّحْمٰنِ الرَّحِيمِ

اَللهُ لاَ إِلٰهَ إِلاَّ هُوَ الْحَىُّ الْقَيُّومُ لاَ تَأْخُذُهُ سِنَةٌ وَلاَ نَوْمٌ
لَهُ مَا فِى السَّمٰوَاتِ وَمَا فِى الْأَرْضِ مَنْ ذَا الَّذِى يَشْفَعُ
عِنْدَهُ إِلاَّ بِإِذْنِهِ يَعْلَمُ مَا بَيْنَ أَيْدِيهِمْ وَمَا خَلْفَهُمْ
وَلاَ يُحِيطُونَ بِشَىْءٍ مِنْ عِلْمِهِ إِلاَّ بِمَا شَآءَ وَسِعَ
كُرْسِيُّهُ السَّمٰوَاتِ وَالْأَرْضَ وَلاَ يَؤُدُهُ حِفْظُهُمَا
وَهُوَ الْعَلِىُّ الْعَظِيمُ ۞

In the Name of Allah, the All-Merciful, the All-Compassionate

255. *Allah, there is no deity but He; the All-Living, the Self-Subsisting (by Whom all subsist). Slumber does not seize Him, nor sleep. His is all that is in the heavens and all that is on the earth. Who is there that will intercede with Him save by His leave? He knows what lies before them and what lies after them (what lies in their future and in their past, what is known to them and what is hidden from them); and they do not comprehend anything of His Knowledge save what He wills. His Seat (of dominion) embraces the heavens and the earth, and the preserving of them does not weary Him; He is the All-Exalted, the Supreme.*

SUBHÂNAKA

$$\text{سُبْحَانَكَ اللّٰهُمَّ وَبِحَمْدِكَ وَتَبَارَكَ اسْمُكَ}$$

$$\text{وَتَعَالَى جَدُّكَ (وَجَلَّ ثَنَاؤُكَ) وَلاَ إِلٰهَ غَيْرُكَ}$$

*"Glory be to You, O Allah, and to You is the praise.
Blessed is Your Name and most high is Your honor. There
is no deity besides You"*

AT-TAHIYYÂT

اَلتَّحِيَّاتُ لِلّٰهِ وَالصَّلَوَاتُ وَالطَّيِّبَاتُ ۞

اَلسَّلَامُ عَلَيْكَ أَيُّهَا النَّبِيُّ وَرَحْمَةُ اللهِ وَبَرَكَاتُهُ ۞

اَلسَّلَامُ عَلَيْنَا وَعَلٰى عِبَادِ اللهِ الصَّالِحِينَ ۞ أَشْهَدُ أَنْ لَا إِلٰهَ إِلَّا اللهُ ۞

وَأَشْهَدُ أَنَّ مُحَمَّدًا عَبْدُهُ وَرَسُولُهُ ۞

Eternity and all dominion is Allah's, and from Him are all blessings and benedictions. Peace be upon you O the {greatest} Prophet, and Allah's mercy and gifts. Peace be also upon us and Allah's righteous servants. I bear witness that there is no deity but Allah, and I also bear witness that Muhammad is His servant and Messenger.

SALAWÂT - 1

اَللّٰهُمَّ صَلِّ عَلَى سَيِّدِنَا مُحَمَّدٍ وَعَلَى أَلِ سَيِّدِنَا مُحَمَّدٍ

كَمَا صَلَّيْتَ عَلَى إِبْرَاهِيمَ وَعَلَى أَلِ إِبْرَاهِيمَ

إِنَّكَ حَمِيدٌ مَجِيدٌ

*"O Allah, bestow Your blessings upon our master Muhammad
and the Family of Muhammad, as You bestowed Your blessings upon Abraham and the Family of Abraham. Assuredly,
You are All-Praised, All-Illustrious."*

SALAWÂT - 2

اَللّٰهُمَّ بَارِكْ عَلَى سَيِّدِنَا مُحَمَّدٍ وَعَلَى أَلِ سَيِّدِنَا مُحَمَّدٍ

كَمَا بَارَكْتَ عَلَى إِبْرَاهِيمَ وَعَلَى أَلِ إِبْرَاهِيمَ

إِنَّكَ حَمِيدٌ مَجِيدٌ

*"O Allah, send Your abundant gifts and favors unto our
master Muhammad and the Family of Muhammad, as
You sent them unto Abraham and the Family of Abraham.
Assuredly, You are All-Praised, All-Illustrious."*

RABBANÂ ÂTINÂ

رَبَّنَا اٰتِنَا فِى الدُّنْيَا حَسَنَةً وَفِى الْاٰخِرَةِ حَسَنَةً

وَقِنَا عَذَابَ النَّارِ

"O our Lord! Grant us goodness in this world and in the
Hereafter and protect us from the punishment of the fire.

RABBANÂGHFIRLÎ

رَبَّنَا اغْفِرْ لِى وَلِوَالِدَىَّ وَلِلْمُؤْمِنِينَ يَوْمَ يَقُومُ الْحِسَابِ

O our Lord! Grant forgiveness to me when the Final Day of
Judgment comes, and to my parents and to the believers."

QUNÛT – 1

اَللّٰهُمَّ إِنَّا نَسْتَعِينُكَ وَنَسْتَغْفِرُكَ وَنَسْتَهْدِيكَ

وَنُؤْمِنُ بِكَ وَنَتُوبُ إِلَيْكَ وَنَتَوَكَّلُ عَلَيْكَ

وَنُثْنِى عَلَيْكَ الْخَيْرَ كُلَّهُ نَشْكُرُكَ وَلاَ نَكْفُرُكَ

وَنَخْلَعُ وَنَتْرُكُ مَنْ يَفْجُرُكَ

*"O Allah! We ask You for help, forgiveness, and guidance.
We believe in You and turn to You in repentance for our
sins, and place our trust in You. We praise You by attrib-
uting all good to You, and thank You, and never feel
ingratitude to You. We reject and cut our relations with
those who are in constant rebellion against You."*

QUNÛT – 2

اَللّٰهُمَّ إِيَّاكَ نَعْبُدُ وَلَكَ نُصَلِّى وَنَسْجُدُ
وَإِلَيْكَ نَسْعٰى وَنَحْفِدُ نَرْجُوا رَحْمَتَكَ وَنَخْشٰى عَذَابَكَ
إِنَّ عَذَابَكَ بِالْكُفَّارِ مُلْحِقٌ

"O Allah, You alone do we worship, and we pray and prostrate for You alone. We endeavor in Your way to obtain Your good pleasure and approval. We hope and expect Your Mercy and fear Your chastisement, for Your chastisement is to surround the unbelievers."